ISRAEL'S HOLY DAYS

ISRAEL'S HOLY DAYS

In Type and Prophecy

by

Daniel Fuchs

LOIZEAUX BROTHERS

Neptune, New Jersey

FIRST EDITION, OCTOBER 1985
FIFTH PRINTING, JUNE 1989

Library of Congress Cataloging-in-Publication Data

Fuchs, Daniel, 1911–
    Israel's holy days.

    1. Fasts and feasts in the Bible.   2. Fasts and feasts—
Judaism.   I. Title.
BS680.F37F83   1985   296.4'3   85-13172
ISBN 0-87213-198-X

To Muriel

"far more than rubies" (Proverbs 31:10)

CONTENTS

INTRODUCTION

The LORD said to Moses, "Speak to the Israelites and say to them: 'These are My appointed feasts, the appointed feasts of the LORD, which you are to proclaim as sacred assemblies. There are six days when you may work, but the seventh day is a Sabbath of rest, a day of sacred assembly. You are not to do any work; wherever you live, it is a Sabbath to the LORD' " (Leviticus 23:1-3).

CALENDARS ARE VERY IMPORTANT. The need for a uniform reckoning of time for the ancient Hebrews was apparent.

The complexities of their economic and political intercourse depended upon [a calendar] more and more as they emerged from a tribal to a monarchical organization, and as they broadened their relations with other nations. It was also imperative for the orderly regulation of their religious festivals.[1]

After the Tabernacle was built, God instructed the Hebrews especially on the subject of holy living. These instructions are compiled in the book of Leviticus, the third book of our Bible. The key verse for the entire book is: "I am the LORD who brought you up out of Egypt to be your God; therefore be holy, because I am holy" (Leviticus 11:45).

The book contains explicit instructions for offering of sacrifices, for meeting everyday problems about cleanliness, and for observing Israel's special holidays. Of the twenty-seven chapters in Leviticus, two (chapters 23 and

---

[1]*Interpreter's Dictionary of the Bible*, vol. 1, p. 482.

25) concern Israel's sacred calendar. This indicates how important Israel's sacred calendar is. A famous rabbi expressed it as follows:

> The catechism of the Jew consists of his calendar. On the pinions of time which bear us through life, God has inscribed the eternal words of His soul-inspiring doctrine, making days and weeks, months and years the heralds to proclaim His truths. Nothing would seem more fleeting than these elements of time, but to them God entrusted the care of His holy things, thereby rendering them more imperishable and more accessible than any mouth of priest, any monument, temple, or altar could have done. Priests die, monuments decay, temples and altars fall to pieces, but time remains forever, and every newborn day emerges fresh and vigorous from its bosom.[2]

Chapter 23 of Leviticus is one of the most fascinating and instructive chapters in the Bible. In a short chapter of forty-four verses, God presents the annual sacred feasts of Jerusalem. At first it seems to be just a simple list of Israel's major holidays. But the more one studies the entire Bible, both the Old and New Testaments, the more one realizes that this chapter is more than a list of mere holidays—they are holy days! It is also more than a list of holy days. It is actually an outline of God's calendar from eternity to eternity!

This calendar is not only sacred to the Jews. It is also precious to Christians, to those who "have found the One Moses wrote about in the Law, and about whom the prophets also wrote—Jesus of Nazareth" (John 1:45). When we found Him, we also discovered that the Old Testament and the New Testament are not two books. They are a unity, the Holy Scriptures.

As we study the calendar outlined in Leviticus 23, we will realize that we cannot understand the New Testament without understanding the Old Testament. The converse is also true. We cannot begin to appreciate the Old Testament until we accept the One who is revealed to us in the New Testament, the Lord Jesus Christ.

---

[2]Hirsch, Rabbi Samuel Raphael, *Judaism Eternal*, vol. 1, p.3.

There are seven appointed feasts of the Lord listed in Leviticus 23:

1. The Passover (verses 4-5)
2. The Feast of Unleavened Bread (verses 6-8)
3. The Sheaf of Firstfruits (verses 9-14)
4. The Feast of Pentecost (the Feast of Weeks) (verses 15-21)
5. The Feast of Trumpets (verses 23-25)
6. The Day of Atonement (verses 26-32)
7. The Feast of Tabernacles (verses 33-43)

The Sabbath

The first three verses in Leviticus 23, which precede our list of appointed feasts, show the importance of what can be called the most important day of the sacred calendar, the Sabbath. Contrary to popular notions, the Sabbath was a day of delight. If you take the Sabbath from a Jew, you are robbing him of a precious jewel. The Sabbath was one of God's most precious gifts to Israel. It refers back to God's act of creation before man sinned. "God blessed the seventh day and made it holy, because on it He rested from all the work of creating that He had done" (Genesis 2:3).

That rest was the Lord's own refreshing rest, made known to man, to be shared in by man newly created. The eye of God rested on His holy creation, and was refreshed. (It is a Jewish remark that "whoever does any work on the Sabbath denies the work of creation."[3]

The Seven Feasts

As we carefully analyze the seven appointed feasts in Leviticus 23 (see Table 1), we observe three significant

---

[3]Bonar, Andrew A., *Commentary on the Book of Leviticus*, pp. 396-397.

facts. First, we observe that all of these holy days are frequently mentioned throughout the Old and New Testaments and that they all have both symbolic and prophetic significance. Second, the New Testament clearly teaches that some of these feasts have already been prophetically fulfilled by the Lord Jesus Christ. Third, it is quite evident that even though all of these feasts are prophetic in both the Old and New Testaments, there are still some that have not as yet been fulfilled.

Table 1. The Appointed Feasts of the Lord (Leviticus 23:4-44)

Fulfilled (verses 4-21)	Will Be Fulfilled (verses 23-44)
Passover	Trumpets
Unleavened Bread	Atonement
Firstfruits	Tabernacles
Pentecost	

As we study the prophetic feasts, we also observe that those that have been fulfilled were fulfilled in exactly the same order and at the same time of the year as they are described in Leviticus 23. Because of these truths, we assume that the next feast on Israel's sacred calendar to be fulfilled is the Feast of Trumpets. See Figure 1, a chart by Dr. Henry J. Heydt, which shows in outline form the scope of God's prophetic calendar.[4]

In the following chapters of this book, beginning with the Passover and continuing through to the Feast of Tabernacles, we study these festivals, their history, their present celebration in the synagogue and home, and their prophetic fulfillment. Since there are in the Scriptures other holy days which are observed by the Jewish people, we have included these in chapters 12 and 13. It will be, by God's grace, a rewarding study.

---

[4]Heydt, Dr. Henry J., (unpublished manuscript).

THE MEANING OF THE JEWISH HOLY DAYS
THE SET FEASTS OF JEHOVAH

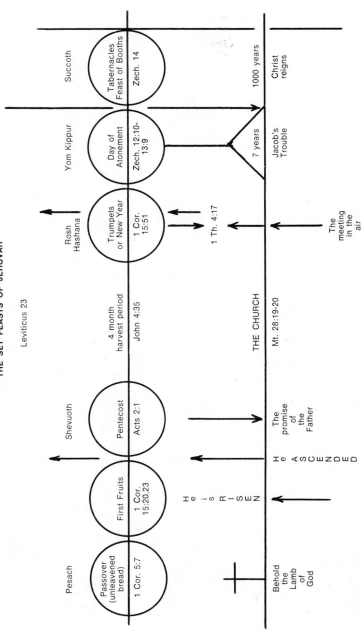

Leviticus 23

Pesach — Passover (unleavened bread) — 1 Cor. 5:7

First Fruits — 1 Cor. 15:20,23

Shevuoth — Pentecost — Acts 2:1

4 month harvest period — John 4:35

Rosh Hashana — Trumpets or New Year — 1 Cor. 15:51

Yom Kippur — Day of Atonement — Zech. 12:10-13:9

Succoth — Tabernacles Feast of Booths — Zech. 14

1 Th. 4:17

7 years — Jacob's Trouble

1000 years — Christ reigns

THE CHURCH — Mt. 28:19-20

Behold the Lamb of God

He is RISEN

He ASCENDED — The promise of the Father

The meeting in the air

1

THE FEAST OF PASSOVER

The LORD said to Moses . . . "These are the LORD's appointed feasts, the sacred assemblies you are to proclaim at their appointed times: The LORD's Passover begins at twilight on the fourteenth day of the first month. On the fifteenth day of that month the LORD's Feast of Unleavened Bread begins; for seven days you must eat bread made without yeast" (Leviticus 23:1,4-6).

ISRAEL'S PROPHETIC CALENDAR opens with the Passover and the Feast of Unleavened Bread. Originally, Passover and Unleavened Bread were quite distinct from each other. Passover took place on the fourteenth of Nisan, and the Feast of Unleavened Bread began on the fifteenth of Nisan and lasted seven days until the twenty-first day of the month. This distinction is clear in Leviticus 23, which, as we have seen, is Israel's prophetic calendar. Leviticus 23:4-6 says:

These are the LORD's appointed feasts, the sacred assemblies you are to proclaim at their appointed times: The LORD's Passover begins at twilight on the fourteenth day of the first month. On the fifteenth day of that month the LORD's Feast of Unleavened Bread begins; for seven days you must eat bread made without yeast.

However, since both feasts are so close to each other (actually the passover lamb, which was slain on the fourteenth of Nisan, could not have been eaten until the fifteenth of Nisan), they are generally treated as one feast both in the Old and New Testaments.

Passover is the most important Jewish festival. It was the first of the three feasts at which all males in Israel were bound to appear before the Lord. For thirty-four hundred years, it has been *the* holy day, the Feast of Redemption.

Passover has a historical setting. On the night of Passover, the Israelites, who had been miraculously preserved, were liberated from slavery and became a nation by the direct intervention of God. It was not only historic, it was also prophetic. Every reader of the New Testament readily recognizes the frequent references to the Exodus, the passover supper, and the Feast of Unleavened Bread. Alfred Edersheim writes about the prophetic significance of the Passover as well as all the feasts.

And that this meaning was intended from the first, not only in reference to the Passover, but to all the feasts, appears from the whole design of the Old Testament, and from the exact correspondence between the types and the antitypes. Indeed it is, so to speak, impressed upon the Old Testament by a law of internal necessity. For when God bound up the future of all nations in the history of Abraham and his seed, He made that history prophetic; and each event and every rite became, as it were, a bud, destined to open in blossom and ripen into fruit on that tree under the shadow of which all nations were to be gathered.[1]

The Passover was prophesied in the Abrahamic covenant. When God promised childless Abram a son, He also prophesied: "Know for certain that your descendants will be strangers in a country not their own, and they will be enslaved and mistreated four hundred years. But I will punish the nation they serve as slaves, and afterward they will come out with great possessions" (Genesis 15:13-14).

In this light, Passover is one of the earliest examples of prophecy that has already been fulfilled in history. It is also an example, as we shall see, of prophecy that is still to be

---

[1]Edersheim, Alfred, *The Temple, Its Ministry and Services*, pp. 178-179.

fulfilled, and as we have already noted, it is one of the most remarkable typological prophecies. It is a type of our Lord Jesus Christ.

The relationship between the Abrahamic covenant and the Passover in Egypt is a fascinating topic for research. For instance, how did Moses know about the Abrahamic covenant? There is no evidence of any written revelation of it before Moses wrote about it. Probably these truths were passed on from generation to generation by word of mouth. If so, it probably was Moses' mother, Jochebed, who taught Moses these truths. In any event, the Abrahamic covenant was the basis of the Passover.

In Exodus 6:2-6,8, God repeats the Abrahamic covenant to Moses:

> God also said to Moses, "I am the LORD. I appeared to Abraham, to Isaac, and to Jacob. . . . I also established My covenant with them to give them the land of Canaan, where they lived as aliens. Moreover, I have heard the groaning of the Israelites, whom the Egyptians are enslaving, and I have remembered My covenant. Therefore, say to the Israelites: 'I am the LORD and I will bring you out from under the yoke of the Egyptians. . . . And I will bring you to the land I swore with uplifted hand to give to Abraham, to Isaac, and to Jacob. I will give it to you as a possession. I am the LORD.' "

As we study the Passover in the Scriptures, we should realize that the Passover in the Old Testament includes two differing yet similar celebrations. Originally, there was the Egyptian Passover and later, what the rabbis have termed the "Permanent Passover."

On the Egyptian Passover, the head of each Jewish household selected either a lamb or a kid of the goats without blemish that was less than a year old. This lamb was selected on the tenth of Nisan and was killed on the eve of the fourteenth. In the original Passover, the blood of this lamb was sprinkled with hyssop on the lintel and the two doorposts of the house. Then the family roasted and ate the whole animal without breaking a bone of it. (If a family was too small to eat an entire lamb, then two families ate together.) All ate the meal, prepared for the journey in the wilderness. This Egyptian Passover was a once-for-all event. It redeemed Israel from slavery. Later, provision was made to keep the Feast of Passover and Unleavened Bread, "at the place the LORD will choose as a dwelling for His Name" (Deuteronomy 16:2). This became the Permanent Passover, which we study in the next chapter.

The story of the Egyptian Passover is found in Exodus 12. The student of the Scriptures should not let the familiarity of this passage keep him or her from continuing to study it over and over again.

Passover, a Sacrifice

The Passover was a sacrifice. Modern theologians dispute this but without any basis. It was an unusual sacrifice. In many respects, it differed from the later sacrifices of the Law, but in some aspects it was similar to what later became the sin offering, combined with the peace offering. It is very important to realize its sacrificial aspect.

The proofs of its sacrificial characteristics are clear and abundant. The details of the selection of the lamb, "year-old males without defect" (Exodus 12:5), the method of sprinkling the blood with hyssop (Exodus 12:22), and the disposal of the remains of the meal (Exodus 12:10), all testify to its sacrificial character. In fact, Moses himself says, "It is the Passover sacrifice to the LORD" (Exodus 12:27).

The purpose of this sacrifice was that the blood of the passover lamb would be sprinkled on the doorposts and the lintels of the Jewish homes, so that the homes would be protected from the destroying angel. It is impossible for any theologian who takes the Scriptures seriously to come to any other conclusion. Exodus 12:13 says, "The blood will be a sign for you on the houses where you are; and when I see the blood, I will pass over you. No destructive plague will touch you when I strike Egypt."

Whether or not one believes in the doctrine of substitution, an objective reader of Exodus 12 must admit that the doctrine is there. The lamb without blemish was carefully chosen and kept four days. Then the head of the family, who was the representative, slew the lamb. When he sprinkled the blood of the lamb upon the doorposts and lintels, he confessed that the family stood in peril of the death angel. He and his family accepted God's means of safety. The result was that he and his family were delivered from bondage. Alexander Maclaren expresses this truth as follows:

> In other words, the Passover is a gospel before the gospel. We are sometimes told that in its sacrificial ideas Christianity is still dressing itself in "Hebrew old clothes." We believe, on the contrary, that the whole sacrificial system of Judaism had for its highest purpose to shadow forth the coming redemption. Christ is not spoken of as "our Passover," because the Mosaic ritual had happened to have that ceremonial; but the Mosaic ritual had that ceremonial mainly because Christ is our Passover, and, by His blood shed on the cross and sprinkled on our consciences, does in spiritual reality that which the Jewish Passover only did in outward form. All other questions about the Old Testament, however interesting and hotly contested, are of secondary importance compared with this. Its chief purpose is to prophesy of Christ.[2]

The Passover was not only a sacrifice, it was a festive meal. It later became the basis of what is known in the Law as the "peace offering." The peace offering was not an offering for peace; it was a meal eaten together by people who were at peace with one another. Later, in the temple days, the peace offering was shared with the priests, who represented God, and the offerer. It became a feast between God and man.

The peace offering always followed the sin offering. It is a picture of our fellowship with our Lord. All of this is typified by the peaceful fellowship which the one who partakes of the passover meal experiences. "But if we walk

---

[2]Maclaren, Alexander, *Expositions on Holy Scripture*, "The Book of Exodus," p. 41.

in the light, as He is in the light, we have fellowship with one another, and the blood of Jesus, His Son, purifies us from every sin" (1 John 1:7).

The passover feast looked forward to "the Lamb of God, who takes away the sin of the world" (John 1:29). "Christ, our Passover lamb, [who] has been sacrificed" (1 Corinthians 5:7), becomes "Christ in you, the hope of glory" (Colossians 1:27).

Passover, a Commemoration

All over the world, the Egyptian Passover is remembered each year in Jewish homes. "This is a day you are to commemorate; for the generations to come you shall celebrate it as a festival to the LORD—a lasting ordinance" (Exodus 12:14). It was celebrated for the first time before deliverance was accomplished. A new calendar was reckoned from it. "This month is to be for you the first month" (Exodus 12:2). The month of the Exodus, from then on, would be the first of the year.

The Passover, a sacrifice; the Passover, a feast; the Passover, a memorial; all became the Passover, a prophecy. "Christ our Passover is sacrificed *for us*" (1 Corinthians 5:7KJV). For us, the past is crowned with His sacrifice. For us, we have fed on the bread of God, and we now live in communion with Him. For us, the memorial of deliverance is celebrated at His table. Here we now eat of the sacrifice as God spoke to the Israelites, "with your cloak tucked into your belt, your sandals on your feet, and your staff in your hand" (Exodus 12:11). We look forward, by His grace, to the time when we all eat with Him in His kingdom. The past, the present, and the future are filled with our Passover Lamb.

2

THE FEAST OF PASSOVER
AND THE LORD'S SUPPER

So they prepared the Passover. When the hour came, Jesus
and His apostles reclined at the table. And He said to them, "I
have eagerly desired to eat this Passover with you before I
suffer" (Luke 22:13-15).

PASSOVER during our Lord's ministry was a festive occa-
sion. At no time in its history was Jerusalem so joyous-
ly thronged with Jews from all over the world. It was
the first of three feasts at which all males living in Israel
must appear before the Lord in the Temple. The other two
were the Feasts of Weeks and Tabernacles, but Passover
had a special fascination. No matter where a Jew lived,
Jerusalem was the holy city. The highest wish of all Jews
everywhere was to walk in the inner court of the Temple
to sacrifice the Passover, to pray, and to listen to the Levitical choir.

In all his wanderings the Jew had not seen a city like his own
Jerusalem. Not Antioch in Asia, not even imperial Rome herself,
excelled it in architectural splendour. Nor has there been, either
in ancient or modern times, a sacred building equal to the Temple, whether for situation or magnificence; nor yet have there
been festive throngs like those joyous hundreds of thousands
who, with their hymns of praise, crowded towards the city on
the eve of a Passover.[1]

---

[1]Edersheim, Alfred, *The Temple, Its Ministry and Services*, p. 6.

Passover was a joyous time for all Israel. From all parts of the land and from all over the world the festive pilgrims came in bands, singing the psalms and bringing with them burnt and peace offerings as the Lord had blessed them. None would appear before the Lord empty-handed. We have no means of definitely knowing how many Jews were in the area of Jerusalem on any given Passover. Josephus said the number of lambs slain at one Passover was 256,000![2] This number seems incredible when we realize that there were at least ten persons for a lamb! In any event, Jerusalem and its environs were besieged by pilgrims from all over the world. Most of these pilgrims camped outside Jerusalem. Every inn in the area was filled to capacity. Those fortunate enough to get lodging in the city were given their accommodations without any cost. In return, they left the skins of their passover lambs and the vessels they used during the passover meal.

Every year our Lord's "parents went to Jerusalem for the Feast of the Passover" (Luke 2:41). We know that our Lord Himself kept the passover feast and the Last Supper, which was held in the upper room that had been prepared and made ready by the owner for Him (Mark 14:12-16).

The pilgrims didn't go to Jerusalem just to pray! It was also a wonderful business opportunity. Merchants from all over the world offered spices, herbs, and condiments. Jerusalem was always a thriving marketplace, but especially at Passover. The markets were jammed with pilgrims. It was at the cattle market, however, where the sheep and goats were driven to the market and put up for sale that the crowds were largest and the bedlam was greatest.

It was customary for the Roman procurator to travel from Caesarea to Jerusalem weeks before Passover to prepare for any uprising that might occur. His headquarters were in Herod's palace, which was actually a wall-encircled fortress with towers and ramparts.

---

[2]Josephus, *Wars VI*, 9.3.

Preparations for the Passover

Preparations for Passover began one month earlier on the fifteenth of Adar when bridges and roads were repaired for the use of the pilgrims. Two weeks before Passover (as well as two weeks before Pentecost and Tabernacles), the flocks were tithed, and temple treasury chests were publicly opened and emptied. We learn from John 11:55 that "When it was almost time for the Jewish Passover, many went up from the country to Jerusalem for their ceremonial cleansing before the Passover." We believe that Paul was applying this custom to our Lord's Supper when he said in 1 Corinthians 11:27-28, "whoever eats the bread or drinks the cup of the Lord in an unworthy manner will be guilty of sinning against the body and blood of the Lord. A man ought to examine himself before he eats of the bread and drinks of the cup."

In the homes, special preparations for Passover began on the evening of the thirteenth of Nisan. (Since the day was always reckoned from evening to evening, this was actually the start of the fourteenth of Nisan.) At this time, the father of the household lighted a wax taper, took a spoon and a brush of several feathers, and carefully searched out and removed all leaven from the home. This search was made in complete silence. Paul referred to this custom in 1 Corinthians 5:7: "Get rid of the old yeast that you may be a new batch without yeast—as you really are. For Christ, our Passover Lamb, has been sacrificed." Rabbinic tradition interprets this custom prophetically according to Zephaniah 1:12 when God "will search Jerusalem with lamps." Many Jewish translations use the word "candles."

Next on the agenda was the selection of the passover lamb. It must be free from any blemish and at least eight days old but not more than one year old. It could not be eaten by an individual alone. There had to be at least ten but no more than twenty in a group. The group at the Lord's passover supper consisted of our Lord and His disciples. While our Lord tarried outside Jerusalem with the other disciples, Peter and John were sent to prepare the

Passover. We don't know where they purchased the lamb before they joined the festive pilgrims, some of whom were leading, others carrying, the sheep to be sacrificed.

Passover in the Temple

The first of three divisions of the worshipers were then admitted to the court of the priests. Then the massive gates were closed behind them, after which the Levites sounded a threefold blast and the sacrifices began. It was an impressive scene. The priests stood in two rows, the priests in each row holding gold and silver bowls. As each Israelite slew the lamb, its blood was caught up by a priest, who handed it to a colleague, receiving in return an empty bowl. When each bowl reached the priest at the altar, he threw it at the base of the altar. Throughout the sacrifice, the Levitical choir led the people in singing Psalms 113 through 118. This was called the Egyptian Hallel (hallel means "praise" in Hebrew and Egyptian refers to the deliverance from Egypt experienced on the first Passover). The psalms were sung antiphonally; that is, the choir sang the first line and the worshipers responded.

Psalm 113 began:

> Choir: "Hallelu Yah" Praise the Lord.
> People: "Hallelu Yah" Repetition of above.
> Choir: "Praise, O servants of the Lord."
> People: "Praise the name of the Lord," and so forth.

It was a hallelujah chorus! If the entire Hallel was completed before the sacrifices of a division were finished, the Hallel was repeated a second or even a third time. The first division was then dismissed, and the second entered. The same ritual was repeated, and then once more for the final division, which was called "lazybones." When the whole service was concluded, incense was burned, the lamps trimmed for the night, and the priests cleaned up the court.

As the sun descended on Jerusalem, thousands and thousands of Jews rushed from the Temple through the streets of Jerusalem bearing the slain lamb carefully wrapped in its own skin. As darkness descended on the city, Peter and John passed courtyards of homes as the owners lighted passover ovens, portable clay stoves. They could smell the fragrance of the sheep, spitted on fragrant pomegranate wood, roasting in the ovens. Relatives and friends from all over the world were gathering together. The rich invited the poor to celebrate the Passover, since they were all poor at the Passover in Egypt. All partake, rich and poor, bond or free, the aged and little children.

It was probably as the sun was beginning to decline in the horizon that Jesus and the other ten disciples descended once more over the Mount of Olives into the holy city. Before them lay Jerusalem in her festive attire. All around, pilgrims were hastening towards it. White tents dotted the sward, gay with the bright flowers of early spring, or peered out from the gardens and the darker foliage of the olive plantations. From the gorgeous temple buildings, dazzling in their snow-white marble and gold, on which the slanting rays of the sun were reflected, rose the smoke of the altar of burnt offering. These courts were now crowded with eager worshipers, offering for the last time, in the real sense, their paschal lambs. The streets must have been thronged with strangers and the flat roofs covered with eager gazers, who either feasted their eyes with a first sight of the sacred city for which they had so often longed, or else once more rejoiced in view of the well-remembered localities. It was the last day-view which the Lord had of the holy city, till His resurrection! Only once more in the approaching night of His betrayal was He to look upon it in the pale light of the full moon. He was going forward to "accomplish His death" in Jerusalem; to fulfill type and prophecy, and to offer Himself up as the true Passover Lamb, "the Lamb of God, which taketh away the sin of the world."[3]

During our Lord's ministry, as the guests gathered around the passover table, they no longer came as at the Egyptian Passover with their cloaks tucked into their belts, their sandals on their feet, and their staff in their hands. On the

---

[3]Edersheim, Alfred, *The Temple, Its Ministry and Services*, pp. 194-195.

contrary, at the Passover they wore their holiday garments as children of the King. In the *Mishnah,* which is the earliest record of Jewish ordinances, the paschal supper was originally very simple. Gamaliel, who was Paul's teacher, said, "Whoever does not explain three things in the Passover has not fulfilled the duty incumbent on him. These three things are: the passover lamb, the unleavened bread, and the bitter herbs. The passover lamb means that God passed over the blood-sprinkled place on the houses of our fathers in Egypt; the unleavened bread means that our fathers were delivered out of Egypt (in haste); and the bitter herbs means that the Egyptians made bitter the lives of our fathers in Egypt" (Pesach 10:15).

A cup of wine was poured for each one in the company. And then our Lord "gave thanks." The rabbinic formula for this thanksgiving was:

Blessed art Thou, Lord our God, who hast created the fruit of the vine! Blessed art Thou, Lord our God, King of the universe, who hast chosen us from among all people, and exalted us from among all languages, and sanctified us with Thy commandments! And Thou hast given us, O Lord our God, in love, the solemn days for joy, and the festivals and appointed seasons for gladness; and this, the day of the Feast of Unleavened Bread, the season of our freedom, a holy convocation, the memorial of our departure from Egypt.[4]

The first cup of wine was then drunk. It was at this first cup that our Lord said: "Take this and divide it among you. For I tell you I will not drink again of the fruit of the vine until the kingdom of God comes" (Luke 22:17-18).

After the first cup, each one washed his hands. The customary prayer for the washing of the hands is: "Blessed art Thou, O Lord our God, who hast sanctified us with Thy commandments and has enjoined us concerning the washing of our hands." It was evidently at this time that our Lord "got up from the meal, took off His outer clothing, and wrapped a towel around His waist" (John 13:4). He then proceeded to wash and dry the disciples' feet.

---

[4]Ibid., pp. 204-205.

The bitter herbs, unleavened bread, the *charoseth,* and the meat of the *chagigah* were then brought in. The *charoseth,* according to one source, was vinegar and water; others say that it was a mixture of vinegar, figs, almonds, dates, and spices that was beaten until it had the consistency of clay or mortar. This was to commemorate the toil of the Israelites when they were enslaved by their Egyptian taskmasters. The *chagigah* was a special voluntary peace offering that was offered at Passover and other festivals.

After this, our Lord took a portion of the bitter herbs in His hand, dipped it into the *charoseth,* and, after thanking God, ate a small piece and gave a similar one to each partaker, who, according to custom, reclined on couches around the table with Him. In this way, our Lord told John, who was reclining next to Him, who would betray Him: "It is the one to whom I will give this piece of bread when I have dipped it in the dish" (John 13:26).

The unleavened bread was then passed around, and the paschal lamb set before the leader. A second cup of wine was poured and drunk, after which an explanation of the feast was given in accordance with Exodus 12:26-27. "And when your children ask you, 'What does this ceremony mean to you?' then tell them, 'It is the Passover sacrifice to the LORD, who passed over the houses of the Israelites in Egypt and spared our homes when He struck down the Egyptians.' " The first part of the Hallel (hymn of praise) was then sung (Psalms 113 and 114). This was followed by a blessing.

After the Hallel the unleavened bread and the bitter herbs dipped in *charoseth* were eaten. Then the flesh of the *chagigah* was eaten, and after that, the paschal lamb. A third cup of wine was poured and drunk. It was after the paschal lamb was eaten that this third cup of wine was drunk. This was the cup which our Lord connected with His Supper. It is called in rabbinic writings "the cup of blessing" (see 1 Corinthians 10:16).

After this, they drank the fourth cup and then the rest of the Hallel was sung. This consisted of Psalms 115 to 118. This was the hymn referred to in Mark 14:22-26:

While they were eating, Jesus took bread, gave thanks, and broke it, and gave it to His disciples, saying, "Take it; this is My body." Then He took the cup, gave thanks, and offered it to them, and they all drank from it. "This is My blood of the covenant, which is poured out for many," He said to them. "I tell you the truth, I will not drink again of the fruit of the vine until that day when I drink it anew in the kingdom of God." When they had sung a hymn, they went out to the Mount of Olives.

The hymn our Lord sang included the words, "The cords of death entangled me, the anguish of the grave came upon me; I was overcome by trouble and sorrow" (Psalm 116:3). This hymn concluded the passover service as our Lord led the disciples to the Mount of Olives.

Passover: Its New Testament Fulfillment

Soon our Lord would offer up "prayers and petitions with loud cries and tears to the One who could save Him from death" (Hebrews 5:7). So the "Lamb without blemish or defect . . . chosen before the creation of the world" (1 Peter 1:19-20) was selected and willing. In a few hours He would become "the atoning sacrifice for our sins, and not only for ours but also for the sins of the whole world" (1 John 2:2).

3

THE FEAST OF FIRSTFRUITS

T HE FEAST OF FIRSTFRUITS was the third feast Israel celebrated during the passover festival.

"Speak to the Israelites and say to them: 'When you
enter the land I am going to give you and you reap its harvest,
bring to the priest a sheaf of the first grain you harvest. He is
to wave the sheaf before the LORD so it will be accepted on your
behalf; the priest is to wave it on the day after the Sabbath'"
(Leviticus 23:10-11).

Passover week, in the days of the Temple, originally
consisted of three main events: (1) the passover lamb slain
on the fourteenth of Nisan, (2) the Feast of Unleavened
Bread beginning on the fifteenth of Nisan, and (3) the
Offering of Firstfruits on the sixteenth of Nisan.

The Sadducees at the time of our Lord disagreed with
this chronology. Some modern commentators also disagree. The difference is due to a misunderstanding of the
words "on the day after the Sabbath" (Leviticus 23:11). The
word "Sabbath" not only refers to the seventh day of the
week; it also clearly refers to the day of the festivals themselves (see Leviticus 23:24-25, 32, 39). The Sadducees, however, believed that the first sheaf was always offered on the
day following the weekly Sabbath of the passover week.
The testimony of Josephus proves beyond a doubt that the
word "Sabbath" in this instance is the fifteenth of Nisan,
on whatever day of the week it fell.

29

But on the second day of unleavened bread, which is the sixteenth day of the month, they first partake of the fruits of the earth, for before that day they do not touch them.[1]

Firstfruits: The Temple Service

The Feast of Firstfruits was not just a harvest festival. It was an acknowledgment of God's bounty and providence to Israel. The order of service for the presentation of the firstfruits during temple days is fascinating and instructive. Remember, the day began at sundown. Alfred Edersheim details the order of service:

Already, on the fourteenth of Nisan, the spot whence the first sheaf was to be reaped had been marked out by delegates from the Sanhedrin, by tying together in bundles, while still standing, the barley that was to be cut down. Though, for obvious reasons, it was customary to choose for this purpose the sheltered Ashes Valley across Kedron, there was no restriction on that point, provided the barley had grown in an ordinary field, of course in Palestine itself, and not in garden or orchard land, and that the soil had not been manured nor yet artificially watered. When the time for cutting the sheaf had arrived, that is, on the evening of the fifteenth of Nisan (even though it were a Sabbath), just as the sun went down, three men, each with a sickle and basket, formally set to work. But in order clearly to bring out all that was distinctive in the ceremony, they first asked of the bystanders three times each of these questions: "Has the sun gone down?" "With this sickle?" "Into this basket?" "On this Sabbath (or first passover day)?" and lastly, "Shall I reap?" Having each time been answered in the affirmative, they cut down barley to the amount of one ephah, or ten omers, or three seahs, which is equal to about three pecks and three pints of our English measure. The ears were brought into the court of the Temple, and thrashed out with canes or stalks, so as not to injure the corn; then "parched" on a pan perforated with holes, so that each grain might be touched by the fire, and finally exposed to the wind. The corn thus prepared was ground in a barley mill, which left the hulls whole. According to some, the flour was always successively passed through thirteen sieves, each closer than the

---

[1]Josephus, *Antiquities of the Jews*, Book 3, X, 5.

other. The statement of a rival authority, however, seems more rational—that it was only done till the flour was sufficiently fine, which was ascertained by one of the *Gizbarim* (treasurers) plunging his hands into it, the sifting process being continued so long as any of the flour adhered to the hands. Though one ephah, or ten omers, of barley was cut down, only one omer of flour, or about 5.1 pints of our measure, was offered in the Temple on the second paschal, or sixteenth day of Nisan.[2]

By the consecration of the firstfruits, the people of Israel joyfully proclaimed that they not only offered the firstfruits to the Lord, but that the whole harvest belonged to Him.

Firstfruits: Its New Testament Fulfillment

The New Testament tells of another harvest.

"But Christ has indeed been raised from the dead, the firstfruits of those who have fallen asleep. For since death came through a man, the resurrection of the dead comes also through a man. For as in Adam all die, so in Christ all will be made alive. But each in his own turn: Christ, the firstfruits; then, when He comes, those who belong to Him" (1 Corinthians 15:20-23).

"Christ has indeed been raised from the dead, the firstfruits of those who have fallen asleep." We rejoice in the fact of our Lord's resurrection. He is risen from the dead. There is a vast difference between the teaching of the immortality of the soul and the resurrection of the body. Paganism gladly accepts the truth of the immortality of the soul, but that is not our hope. Our hope is not in an immortal, disembodied soul. It is in the resurrection of the body. Our Lord really died; His body was buried; He rose from the dead. The body of our Lord, which was resurrected, was the same body that died for us. Since He is the firstfruits of the harvest, so also is the harvest: "But each in his own turn: Christ, the firstfruits; then, when He comes, those who belong to Him" (1 Corinthians 15:23). This truth gives us abundant comfort.

---

[2]Edersheim, Alfred, *The Temple, Its Ministry and Services*, pp. 223-224.

We should be clear in our thinking about the meaning of the word "resurrection" as it applies to the Lord Jesus Christ and as it will apply to believers. It means more than to reanimate, to resuscitate, or to reinvigorate. There were several resurrections before our Lord rose from the dead. In the Old Testament, the Lord heard Elijah's prayer and raised the widow's son from the dead (1 Kings 17:17-23). In the New Testament, our Lord raised from the dead the daughter of Jairus (Luke 8:41-56), the son of the widow of Nain (Luke 7:11-15), and Lazarus (John 11:43-44).

There is a remarkable study in contrasts concerning these three resurrections found in the New Testament. The body of each was in a different condition. The girl appeared to be sleeping; the young man was being carried to his grave, decay already begun in the warm climate; Lazarus had been dead four days and decay was advanced. Our Lord used a different method in each case: He took the little girl by her hand; He didn't touch the body of the young man, He touched the bier which was bearing him to the grave; and He cried to Lazarus with a loud voice. His care for each was different: He fed the girl; He gave the son to his mother; and He had Lazarus released from his grave-clothes. Here the contrasts end. The comparisons are equally vivid: they were all dead, they were all raised from the dead, it was our Lord who raised them, and *they all died again*. Our Lord's resurrection was different. He rose to die no more! "Christ, the firstfruits; then, when He comes, those who belong to Him."

The contrasts and comparisons between our Lord's resurrection and that of Lazarus are especially instructive. The stone had to be rolled away to let Lazarus come out of the tomb. The angel rolled the stone away from our Lord's tomb, not to let the Lord out, but to permit the disciples to enter. Lazarus "came out, his hands and feet wrapped with strips of linen, and a cloth around his face" (John 11:44), and the disciples had to take off the graveclothes and let him go. How different it was with the resurrection of our Lord! He is the Prince of Life. It was utterly impossible that He should be holden of death. He arose. And although His body had been bound by graveclothes, neither the graveclothes, nor the walls of the tomb, nor the walls of the room could confine His glorious body. It is His resurrection that comforts us in our sorrow. "Because He lives, we too shall live."

It was "after the Sabbath, at dawn on the first day of the week, [when] Mary Magdalene and the other Mary went to look at the tomb" (Matthew 28:1) and learned that the Lord Jesus Christ had indeed been raised from the dead and become the firstfruits of those who belong to Him. The firstfruits were representative of the entire harvest. There is yet to be another harvest: "Christ, the firstfruits; then, when He comes, those who belong to Him" (1 Corinthians 15:23). Our faith in the future is not in philosophical vagaries concerning the "immortality of the soul." It is firmly embedded in the fact of our Lord's resurrection. The resurrection of the believer is not patterned after that of Lazarus. We shall be raised in our Lord's likeness.

It is human for us to wonder about the resurrection body of our loved ones. With what body will they be raised? He is the firstfruits. Like Him, the resurrection bodies of our loved ones (and ours too) will be the same bodies that were buried in the grave, but with splendid differences. They will be our loved ones; we shall see and recognize them. "He will wipe every tear from their eyes. There will be no more death or mourning or crying or pain, for the old order of things has passed away" (Revelation 21:4).

4

THE FEAST OF PENTECOST

The LORD said to Moses, . . . "From the day after the Sabbath, the day you brought the sheaf of the wave offering, count off seven full weeks. Count off fifty days up to the day after the seventh Sabbath, and then present an offering of new grain to the LORD. From wherever you live, bring two loaves made of two-tenths of an ephah of fine flour, baked with yeast, as a wave offering of firstfruits to the LORD. Present with this bread seven male lambs, each a year old and without defect, one young bull and two rams. They will be a burnt offering to the LORD, together with their grain offerings and drink offerings—an offering made by fire, an aroma pleasing to the LORD. Then sacrifice one male goat for a sin offering and two lambs, each a year old, for a fellowship offering. The priest is to wave the two lambs before the LORD as a wave offering, together with the bread of the firstfruits. They are a sacred offering to the LORD for the priest. On that same day you are to proclaim a sacred assembly and do no regular work. This is to be a lasting ordinance for the generations to come, wherever you live" (Leviticus 23:9,15-21).

THE FEAST OF PENTECOST climaxed the glad season of Israel's grain harvest.

The beginning of the grain harvest was marked by the sacrifice, at the sanctuary, of the omer, the first sheaf of the newly cut barley; fifty days later, at the close of the harvest period, two loaves of bread, baked from the wheat of the new crop, were offered as a sacrifice. This bread offering was called the firstfruits of wheat harvest and the festival was therefore also

34

called *Yom ha-Bikkurim,* the day of offering the first loaves of the
new crop to God.[1]

The first omer, which was offered during the Feast of
Unleavened Bread, on the sixteenth of Nisan, was of the
sheaf as it was reaped from the newly grown plants, as
described in Leviticus 23:15-21:

> From the day after the Sabbath, the day you brought the sheaf
> of the wave offering, count off seven full weeks. Count off fifty
> days up to the day after the seventh Sabbath, and then present
> an offering of the new grain to the LORD. From wherever you
> live, bring two loaves made of two-tenths of an ephah of fine
> flour, baked with yeast, as a wave offering of firstfruits to the
> LORD. Present with this bread seven male lambs, each a year old
> and without defect, one young bull and two rams. They will be
> a burnt offering to the LORD, together with their grain offerings
> and drink offerings—an offering made by fire, an aroma pleas-
> ing to the LORD. Then sacrifice one male goat for a sin offering
> and two lambs, each a year old, for a fellowship offering. The
> priest is to wave the two lambs before the LORD as a wave
> offering, together with the bread of the firstfruits. They are a
> sacred offering to the LORD for the priest. On that same day you
> are to proclaim a sacred assembly and do no regular work. This
> is to be a lasting ordinance for the generations to come, wherev-
> er you live.

Pentecost and the Giving of the Law

"The day after the Sabbath" the "sheaf of the first grain"
(Leviticus 23:10) was offered on the sixteenth of Nisan.
From that date, fifty days were counted and usually the
sixth day of the Hebrew month Sivan is proclaimed as
Shavuoth (a Hebrew word meaning "weeks") or Feast of
Weeks or Pentecost. This chronology is fascinating because
it is the basis of the rabbinic reason why Judaism now
celebrates the giving of the Law on the Day of Pentecost.
Dr. Alfred Edersheim gives insight to this reasoning:

---

[1]Schauss, Hayyim, *The Jewish Festivals,* pp. 86-87.

The "feast of unleavened bread" may be said not to have quite passed till fifty days after its commencement, when it merged in that of Pentecost, or "of Weeks." According to unanimous Jewish tradition, which was universally received at the time of Christ, the day of Pentecost was the anniversary of the giving of the Law on Mount Sinai, which the Feast of Weeks was intended to commemorate. Thus, as the dedication of the harvest, commencing with the presentation of the first omer on the Passover, was completed in the thank offering of the two wave loaves at Pentecost, so the memorial of Israel's deliverance appropriately terminated in that of the giving of the Law, just as, making the highest application of it, the Passover sacrifice of the Lord Jesus may be said to have been completed in the outpouring of the Holy Spirit on the day of Pentecost. Jewish tradition has it, that on the second of the third month, or Sivan, Moses had ascended the mount, that he communicated with the people on the third, reascended the mount on the fourth, and that then the people sanctified themselves on the fourth, fifth, and sixth of Sivan, on which latter day the Ten Commandments were actually given them. Accordingly, the days before Pentecost were always reckoned as the first, second, third, etc., since the presentation of the omer. Thus Maimonides beautifully observes: "Just as one who is expecting the most faithful of his friends is wont to count the days and hours to his arrival, so we also count from the omer of the day of our Exodus from Egypt to that of the giving of the Law, which was the object of our Exodus, as it is said: 'I bare you on eagle's wings, and brought you unto Myself.' And because this great manifestation did not last more than one day, therefore we annually commemorate it only one day."[2]

We can see that, even though Scriptures do not say that Pentecost is the actual anniversary of the giving of the Law on Mt. Sinai, there is compelling evidence that indicates that "when the day of Pentecost came" as described in Acts 2:1, God's revelation on Mt. Sinai was probably in the minds of the apostles when "suddenly a sound like the blowing of a violent wind came from heaven and filled the whole house where they were sitting" (Acts 2:2).

A modern Orthodox Hebraist scholar describes the giving of the Law:

---

[2]Edersheim, Alfred, *The Temple, Its Ministry and Services*, pp. 225-226.

The Revelation on Mt. Sinai

Dawn of the sixth day of Sivan, in the year 2448 after the creation of the world . . . thunder and lightning rent the air, and the sound of the shofar was heard growing strangely louder and louder. All the people in the camp of Israel trembled.

Then all was quiet again. The air was very still. Not a sound was to be heard. No bird twittered, no donkey brayed, no ox lowed. Every living thing held its breath. Even the angels interrupted their heavenly praises. Everybody and everything kept silent . . . waiting. . . .

Suddenly G-d's mighty words were heard from one corner of the earth to the other:

"I AM G-D THY G-D!"

One after another, G-d proclaimed the Ten Commandments.[3]

Pentecost: Its Old Testament Offerings

On Pentecost, many different offerings were presented in the Temple. After the regular morning sacrifice, there was a burnt offering of "seven male lambs, each a year old and without defect, one young bull and two rams" (Leviticus 23:18). This was followed by a meal offering and a drink offering. After that, there was a sin offering of one kid, and then the climactic offering of the day, a "fellowship" or "peace" offering of "two lambs, each a year old" waved before the Lord, together with the two loaves which had been baked with leaven. (See Leviticus 23:17,19). This peace offering was *not* offered on the altar; it was given to the priest. It could not be placed on the altar, because the loaves were baked with leaven.

It is highly significant that the sin offering preceded the peace offering. We will never understand the meaning of the peace offering until we grasp this truth. The sin offering came first, then the peace offering. The peace offering was not an offering for peace. It is a heartfelt thank offering of one who has peace with his Lord. It is a sacramental meal where God, who is represented by the priest, eats a meal

[3]Mindel, Nissan, *Complete Festival Series*, p. 167.

together with His children, who have already been cleansed from their sin. It should be observed that the two loaves, together with the two lambs which were offered at Pentecost, were the only public peace offerings that were celebrated by Israel. The peace offering of Pentecost was a feast of fellowship and peace between God and His redeemed people.

Pentecost: Its New Testament Fulfillment

Was Pentecost, like Passover, Unleavened Bread, and Firstfruits, also prophetic? The New Testament is abundantly clear that it was. Our Lord Jesus Christ, having fulfilled the type of the passover lamb at Calvary, when the corn of wheat was planted in the ground, rose from the dead and became the "firstfruits," fulfilling the type of the wave sheaf on the "day after the Sabbath." Then fifty days were counted, and "when the day of Pentecost came, they were all together in one place. Suddenly a sound like the blowing of a violent wind came from heaven and filled the whole house where they were sitting" (Acts 2:1-2).

If Jewish tradition connected the "feast of firstfruits" with the "mount that might be touched," and the "voice of words which they that heard entreated that the word should not be spoken to them any more," we have in this respect also "come unto Mount Zion," and to the better things of the new covenant. To us the Day of Pentecost is, indeed, the "feast of firstfruits," and that of the giving of the better law, "written not in tables of stone, but on the fleshy tables of the heart," "with the Spirit of the living God." For, as the worshipers were in the Temple, probably just as they were offering the wave lambs and the wave bread, the multitude heard that "sound from heaven, as of a mighty rushing wind," which drew them to the house where the apostles were gathered, there to hear "every man in his own language" [proclaiming] "the wonderful works of God." And on that Pentecost day, from the harvest of firstfruits, not less than three thousand souls added to the Church were presented as a wave offering to the Lord. The cloven tongues of fire and the apostolic gifts of that day of firstfruits have, indeed, long since disappeared. But the mighty rushing sound of the Presence and Power of the Holy Ghost has gone forth into all the world.[4]

---

[4]Edersheim, Alfred, *The Temple, Its Ministry and Services*, p. 231.

5

A STRANGE HIATUS:
LEVITICUS AND RUTH

The LORD said to Moses . . . "When you reap the harvest of your land, do not reap to the very edges of your field or gather the gleanings of your harvest. Leave them for the poor and the alien. I am the LORD your God" (Leviticus 23:9,22).

A HIATUS is a break or interruption in the continuity of a work. We have been studying Israel's sacred calendar of feasts in chapter 23 of Leviticus. These included: (1) the Feasts of Passover and Unleavened Bread (verses 4-8), (2) the Sheaf of Firstfruits (verses 9-14), and (3) the Feast of Pentecost (verses 15-21).

In verse 22, there is a change in subject matter. After minutely describing these feasts, which are in the late spring, there is a verse that seems to have absolutely nothing to do with Israel's sacred holy days: "When you reap the harvest of your land, do not reap to the very edges of your field or gather the gleanings of your harvest. Leave them for the poor and the alien. I am the LORD your God." These are strange words in a strange place. The author then returns to the sacred feasts.

All of the feasts that follow verse 22 occur in the fall of the year, the seventh month of Israel's calendar: (4) the Feast of Trumpets (verses 23-25), (5) the Day of Atonement (verses 26-32), and (6) the Feast of Tabernacles (verses 33-43). There is no holy day during the summer months.

In previous chapters, as we carefully analyzed these seven "appointed feasts," we observed three significant facts. In the first place, all of these days are mentioned frequently throughout the Scriptures, in the Old and New Testaments, and they all have significant symbolic and prophetic meaning. Secondly, the New Testament clearly teaches that some of these feasts have already been fulfilled prophetically; these are readily recognized as those occurring in the spring of the year. Thirdly, it is evident that even though all of the feasts are prophetic, there are some that have not as yet been fulfilled. These are those that are celebrated in the fall, Israel's seventh month. They are the Feasts of Trumpets, Atonement, and Tabernacles.

God's Provision for All Peoples on Earth

Between the fulfilled feasts of verses 4 through 21 and the unfulfilled feasts of verses 23 through 44, there is a gap that lasts several months. Most of Israel's feasts are agricultural, and during the long summer months the fields are white unto harvest. As they reap the harvest in these months, the Israelites are commanded not to keep all of the fruits for themselves and are admonished to leave enough of the bounty to share with the poor and the alien. God's provisions are not only for Israel. In God's providence, Israel is to feed the poor and the alien also, just as the gospel is to the Jew first and also to the Greek (Gentile).

If this provision had not been made, we could never have the book of Ruth. The story of Ruth is more than a beautiful idyll, more than a love story; it is a revelation of God's heart. It is God's missionary program.

It has always been God's will that all men everywhere would love, honor, and worship Him. When man failed at Babel, God chose the family of Abraham so that "all peoples on earth will be blessed through [him]" (Genesis 12:3). God's blessing was to be universal, to the family of Abraham first, but also to "all peoples on earth."

The book of Ruth is set historically between the book of Judges, when "Israel had no king [and] everyone did as

he saw fit" (Judges 21:25), and the book of First Samuel,
when Saul is anointed and crowned as king and the kingdom is established. It is not stretching the facts to say that
Leviticus 23:22 and its typological counterpart, the book
of Ruth, are a hiatus between human failure on the one
side and the glory of the kingdom on the other.

The story of the book of Ruth is so familiar that it is not
necessary to repeat it. Ruth, the chief character, is a
Moabitess, a Gentile.

She who was cursed by the law becomes married to Boaz and,
as we learn from the ending, Ruth is the great-grandmother of
David. Her name appears therefore in the first chapter of the
New Testament in the list of ancestors of Him who is David's Son
and David's Lord. She is the third Gentile woman in the genealo-
gy of our Lord. The two Canaanitish women, Tamar and Rahab,
precede her. The promises made to Abraham, that the Gentiles
were to receive blessing through his seed, are confirmed through
the history of these Gentile women among the ancestors of
David and our Lord.[1]

Because of the Levitical provision for the poor and the
stranger, a cursed Moabitess met her kinsman redeemer
and became the ancestor not only of David but of our
Lord. Under the Law, a Gentile had to become a proselyte
to partake of Israel's blessings—not so under grace.

Salvation for the Gentiles: New Testament Fulfillment

"When the day of Pentecost came . . . there were staying
in Jerusalem God-fearing Jews from every nation under
heaven" (Acts 2:1,5). It was then that the firstfruits of Israel's ripened harvest were presented to the Lord. At that
time the sheaves were reaped from Israel itself. All of the
three thousand people who accepted the Lord on the Day
of Pentecost were "God-fearing Jews from every nation
under heaven" (Acts 2:5). Many of these Jews were prose-

[1]Gaebelein, A.C., *The Annotated Bible*, "Ruth," p. 118; *Gaebelein's Concise Commentary on the Whole Bible*, p. 232.

lytes, Gentiles who had converted to Judaism. When they returned to their homes, they shared the gospel not only with their Jewish neighbors but with their Gentile friends. Salvation was literally "first for the Jew, then for the Gentile" (Romans 1:16).

Thus we see it was God's eternal purpose that there was abundant fruit left for "the poor and the alien" from every land, and soon millions were brought in who had been "excluded from citizenship in Israel and foreigners to the covenants of the promise, without hope and without God in the world. But now in Christ Jesus [they] who once were far away have been brought near through the blood of Christ. For He Himself is our peace, who has made the two one and has destroyed the barrier, the dividing wall of hostility" (Ephesians 2:12-14). Like Ruth of old, millions of souls have gleaned in the fields of Bethlehem and have found their Kinsman Redeemer.

There is still abundant provision for all in that Feast of Pentecost harvest. But the summer has been long. For nineteen centuries our Lord has reaped an abundant harvest of Jews and Gentiles, but He has other festivals on His calendar. Our ears long to hear the sound of the coming Feast of Trumpets.

6

THE FEAST OF TRUMPETS

The LORD said to Moses, "Say to the Israelites: 'On the first day of the seventh month you are to have a day of rest, a sacred assembly commemorated with trumpet blasts. Do no regular work, but present an offering made to the LORD by fire' " (Leviticus 23:23-25).

THE MOST SOLEMN HOLY DAYS of Israel's sacred calendar are celebrated in the month of Tishri, the seventh (sabbatic) month of the year. These solemn, sacred convocations include the Feast of Trumpets and the Day of Atonement. In modern Judaism, these are usually called "the days of awe." During this climactic month, the Feast of Tabernacles, which is the most jubilant event of Israel's year, is also celebrated. The month of Tishri usually falls in late September and early October.

In previous chapters, we studied the prophetic message of Israel's sacred calendar as outlined in Leviticus 23. We observed that Israel's holy days fall into two groups— those celebrated in the spring and those kept in autumn. As already mentioned, all of these feasts are prophetic, but some of the prophecies have already been fulfilled, as is clearly taught in the New Testament. The others are still unfulfilled prophetically.

The prophetic feasts that have already been fulfilled are those that are kept in the springtime (Leviticus 23:4-21). These feasts include Passover and Unleavened Bread (Leviticus 23:4-8; 1 Corinthians 5:7; 1 Peter 1:19-20), Firstfruits (Leviticus 23:9-14; 1 Corinthians 15:23; 1 Thessalonians 4:13-18), and Pentecost (Leviticus 23:15-21; Acts 2:1-40).

On the Day of Pentecost, two loaves baked with leaven were offered as a fellowship or peace offering (Ephesians 2:14). At Firstfruits, it was a sheaf of separate growths loosely bound together that was offered. At Pentecost, it was loaves that were offered, a real union of the grains of wheat that made one harmonious body.

The Feast of Pentecost closed Israel's springtime festivals. After Pentecost, there were four long summer months, during which harvests were reaped before the next holy day, which was the Feast of Trumpets. Leviticus 23:23-25 says, "The LORD said to Moses, 'Say to the Israelites: "On the first day of the seventh month you are to have a day of rest, a sacred assembly commemorated with trumpet blasts. Do no regular work, but present an offering made to the LORD by fire." ' "

We are now faced with a surprising fact. The Scriptures call for "a sacred assembly commemorated with trumpet blasts," but instead the Jewish calendar celebrates New Year's Day, Rosh Hashanah, on that day! This is not just a question of which day is New Year's Day. It is evident that ancient Israel kept at least two calendars (the rabbis mention four): the civil calendar, which began in Nisan, and the religious calendar, which began in Tishri. Modern Judaism has, at some time since the writing of the Pentateuch, formulated a system that, while adapting some of the Scriptures to its tenets, also differs from them. This is a fact that both Jewish and Christian scholars accept.

Historians write of "the religion of Israel" as revealed in the Pentateuch, and of Judaism, which can also be defined as the religion of Israel as explained in the Talmud. The difference between the two "religions" is the watershed that divides Hebrew Christians from their brethren. We Jews who have accepted the Lord Jesus Christ as our Messiah insist that we are biblical Jews. "We have found the One Moses wrote about in the Law, and about whom the prophets also wrote—Jesus of Nazareth, the son of Joseph" (John

1:45). The Scriptures reveal Him; the tradition of the elders hides Him.

One of the best known Jewish New Year's Day customs is the expression of the greeting, "May you be inscribed for a good year!" This greeting is based on the belief that God judges the world on Rosh Hashanah. The rabbis believe that the first of Tishri is the date of creation. The *Mishnah* (the written code of the oral law) speaks of it as a day of judgment when all men pass before the Creator as sheep are examined by the shepherd. *The Jewish Encyclopedia* describes the scene:

> God seated on His throne to judge the world . . . openeth the Book of Records; it is read, every man's signature being found therein. The great trumpet is sounded; a still, small voice is heard; the angels shudder, saying, "This is the day of judgment": for His very ministers are not pure before God. As a shepherd mustereth his flock, causing them to pass under his rod, so doth God cause every living soul to pass before Him, to fix the limit of every creature's life and to foreordain its destiny. On New Year's Day the decree is written; on the Day of Atonement it is sealed who shall live and who are to die, etc. But penitence, prayer and charity may avert the evil decree.[1]

And so for the next ten days between Rosh Hashanah and the Day of Atonement, there are many good deeds and many prayers, but no assurance of forgiveness. Prayers and good deeds are splendid, but because God's way of forgiveness is ignored, the days of awe end "the day" with no atonement.

From this brief description, it can be observed that the modern celebration of Rosh Hashanah is a mixture of biblical truth and paganism. The ancient Babylonians believed that every year all of the gods met in a room in heaven which was called the "room of fate." Marduk, the chief of the gods, presided at this meeting. The minutes of the meeting were kept by Nabu, who was not only the god of wisdom but also the messenger of the gods. He recorded

---

[1]*The Jewish Encyclopedia*, vol. 2, p. 286.

all of mankind's deeds on "the tablets of fate." It was on these tablets that judgment for all was inscribed at the New Year.

There are other similarities between the Babylonian version of New Year's Day and Rosh Hashanah. For instance, we have observed that the rabbis taught that the world was created on Rosh Hashanah. In the New Year services at the temple of Marduk, he was declared the king and the creator of the world. The "high priest" recited the account of the creation of the world in front of an image of Marduk.

The Feast of Trumpets During Temple Times

We do not have much knowledge of how the Feast of Trumpets was celebrated during temple times. According to Alfred Edersheim, trumpets and horns were blown in Jerusalem from morning to evening. These were not the silver trumpets of the priests, but the horns of animals. The *Mishnah* says that the horns of any kind of animals except those of oxen or calves could be used. The reason for this exception was in order not to remind God of the sin of the golden calf. Most frequently used was the ram's horn, which especially alluded to the binding of Isaac when "Abraham looked up and there in a thicket he saw a ram caught by its horns. He went over and took the ram and sacrificed it as a burnt offering instead of his son" (Genesis 22:13).

According to the Jewish commentator, Saadiah Gaon, the blowing of the trumpets reminds Israel of: (1) the Creator; (2) the duty to return to God; (3) the revelation on Mount Sinai; (4) the exhortation of the prophets; (5) the destruction of the Temple; (6) the binding of Isaac for sacrifice; (7) imminent danger; (8) the day of judgment; (9) the redemption of Israel; (10) the resurrection.[2]

[2]Gaon, Saadiah, *The Encyclopedia Judaica*, vol. 14, p. 1447.

The Prophetic Significance to the Feast of Trumpets

Is there a prophetic significance to the Feast of Trumpets (as well as to the Day of Atonement and Tabernacles)? The long prophetic hiatus that began at Pentecost has lasted for almost two thousand years. Myriads of every kingdom, tongue, tribe, and nation have gleaned in the fields of Pentecost. Pentecost was the firstfruits; the complete harvest must yet be gathered. The fields are ripe unto harvest. One day the summer will end, the silence of the long months will be over. In 1 Corinthians 15:51-52 we read: "Listen, I tell you a mystery: We will not all sleep, but we will all be changed—in a flash, in the twinkling of an eye, at the last trumpet. For the trumpet will sound, the dead will be raised inperishable, and we will be changed."

Thus, the next event in God's calendar is the Feast of Trumpets. It is the return of our Lord. We lovingly anticipate Him! But Israel still awaits her day of atonement, her national repentance, and her turning to God.

Students of prophecy will recognize that Leviticus 23 anticipates a pretribulation rapture. As we have seen, the feasts of the spring months, Passover and Unleavened Bread, Firstfruits, and Pentecost, were historically fulfilled in the same order as listed in Leviticus 23. It is consistent to believe that the remainder of these feasts as types will be fulfilled in order. We are today in verse 22 of Leviticus 23. Our great expectation is to hear the trumpet that will sound as the dead are raised incorruptible. Then will come the Day of Atonement, which will occur during the great tribulation, and after that, the Feast of Tabernacles.

7

ROSH HASHANAH OR
NEW YEAR'S DAY

NEW YEAR'S DAY for the Jews is not a holiday, it is a holy day, often called, together with the Day of Atonement, the "days of awe." It is celebrated on the first and second days of Tishri. It is not a time of frivolity but of introspection and prayer. It is a solemn day when Jews believe that all people stand before the Creator.

The Orthodox Jew does not come to this season unprepared. He knows the New Year is approaching. During the preceding month, the month of Elul, which to the modern Jew is the last month of the year according to the civil calendar, the approach of Rosh Hashanah is heralded by the sounding of the shofar in the synagogue. All year long the shofar, which is usually a ram's horn, lies hidden, probably in the holy ark in the synagogue. It is not sounded on the Sabbath. However, on the first day of Elul, it is taken from its hiding place to play a prominent role as Israel's days of awe approach. The sounding of the shofar reaches its crescendo on Rosh Hashanah, when it is sounded after the reading of the Law.

The Sacrifice of Isaac

The reading of the Law on the second day's service is the story of the sacrifice of Isaac. The rabbis believe that the sacrifice of Isaac, when a ram was offered in his stead, took place on New Year's Day. Because of this belief, this story, together with that of Isaac's birth, is the basis of the liturgy of the second day's service in the synagogue.

Because of this, there is no Bible story more familiar to the Orthodox Jew than the story of Abraham offering up Isaac. It abounds in spiritual truth. This story is found in Genesis, chapter 22. It is helpful to study it together with Psalm 22 and Luke 22:42-44.

It is the story of Abraham's faithfulness: "Some time later God *tested* Abraham" (Genesis 22:1). We should realize that God did not *tempt* Abraham, as the Authorized Version states; God *tested* Abraham. When Satan *tempts,* he tries to defeat us. When God *tests,* He provides victory. Nor does God test everyone. C. H. Mackintosh writes concerning Abraham's test:

> However, it is well to see that God confers a signal honor upon us when He thus tests our hearts. We never read that the Lord did tempt Lot. No, Sodom tempted Lot. He never reached a sufficiently high elevation to warrant his being tried by the hand of Jehovah. It was too plainly manifested that there was plenty between his heart and the Lord, and it did not, therefore, require the furnace to bring that out. Sodom would have held out no temptation whatever to Abraham. This was made manifest in his interview with Sodom's king, in chapter 14. God knew well that Abraham loved Him far better than Sodom; but He would make it manifest that he loved Him better than anyone or anything, by laying His hand upon the nearest and dearest object, "Take now thy son, thine only son Isaac."[1]

For many long years Abraham waited for his promised seed. Finally, the Lord gave him a son by Sarah and then commanded him to cast out Ishmael, the son of the bond-woman. That in itself was enough to test any man. It was a test of faith. But Abraham believed God and obeyed Him.

Isaac's birth was in a very real sense miraculous. He was

<hr/>

[1]Mackintosh, C.H., *Notes on Genesis*, pp. 225-226; *Genesis to Deuteronomy*, pp. 95-96.

the seed of Abraham, born after his mother was "past the age of childbearing" (Genesis 18:11). Perhaps Abraham even thought that Isaac was the Messiah. (This is one of the reasons why Jewish couples earnestly desire their firstborn to be a son. They hope he may be the Messiah.) But the promised Messiah was not only to be the seed of Abraham, but also the seed of the woman (Genesis 3:15). Thus we see Jesus, born of a virgin, Mary, who was herself of the seed of Abraham.

Isaac grew into young manhood. Josephus says that Isaac was twenty-seven years old when his father was told to sacrifice him. The Scriptures don't give his exact age, however, but he had grown strong enough to carry the wood that covered the altar that was large enough to bear his body. Thus, he was not a young weakling.

Abraham Believed God

It was when Abraham's only son, the heir to the Abrahamic covenant, the son of promise whom he greatly loved, blossomed into manhood that God ordered Abraham to offer him up as a sacrifice on Mount Moriah. This command did not come from within Abraham, it was not suggested by the human sacrifices of the Canaanites, nor did it come from Satan. It came from the one true God, who was proving Abraham's faith! The final issue clearly showed that God wasn't interested in the death of Isaac. Rather, He wanted Abraham's complete surrender.

You and I know the outcome of Abraham's deep trial. At the time, Abraham did not. He drank the dregs of the bitterness of his sorrow. Imagine the pain these words must have brought to Abraham: "Take your son, your only son Isaac, whom you love" (Genesis 22:2). He laid the wood "on his son" (verse 6). He told Isaac, "God Himself will provide the lamb" (verse 8). Then he "bound his son Isaac" and "took the knife to slay his son" (verses 9-10).

Luther remarked that it must have seemed as if God's promise would fail, or that this command came from Satan, not from God. How beautifully Paul describes Abraham's faith in Romans 4:20-21. "Yet he did not waver through unbelief, [he] was strengthened in his faith, [he was] fully persuaded." But the letter to the Hebrews shows the basic reasoning of Abraham, "that God could raise the dead, and figuratively speaking, he did receive Isaac back from death" (Hebrews 11:19).

Abraham's answer to his great trial was "he believed God." Four centuries before any of the written Word came into existence, God spoke to him, and Abraham implicitly put his trust in God's Word. God commanded Abraham to leave his kindred, Abraham obeyed; God promised him a seed, Abraham believed. For long years Abraham waited for God to fulfill His promise. Finally, Isaac was born. God had fulfilled His promise.

The same God who fulfilled His promise, now demanded that Abraham offer Isaac, his beloved son, as a sacrifice. Abraham believed God and showed his faith by his works. He knew that God honored His Word. As previously mentioned, it is very possible that he even thought that Isaac was the promised Seed of the woman of Genesis 3:15, the Messiah. In any event, Abraham knew that Isaac was his own promised seed. God had said that in his seed "all peoples on earth will be blessed" (Genesis 12:3). Abraham believed and obeyed God.

The key to Abraham's obedience was that he actually believed in the resurrection. If Isaac was the Messiah and the Messiah had to die, then it was necessary for God to raise Him from the dead!

By faith Abraham, when God tested him, offered Isaac as a sacrifice. He who had received the promises was about to sacrifice his one and only son, even though God had said to him, "It is through Isaac that your offspring will be reckoned." Abraham reasoned that God could raise the dead, and figuratively speaking, he did receive Isaac back from death" (Hebrews 11:17-19).

Abraham actually expected God to raise up Isaac from the dead!

Enemies of the gospel complain that the biblical doctrine of justification by faith alone is amoral. Even some well-meaning friends of the gospel frequently teach a "faith-plus-works" salvation. They complain that if righteousness is by faith alone, apart from works of the Law, then a man who is saved by faith could still commit heinous crimes. This could not be if he has the faith of Abraham.

Abraham's faith resulted in acts of obedience. Romans 4:20-24 says;

> Yet he did not waver through unbelief regarding the promise of God, but was strengthened in his faith and gave glory to God, being fully persuaded that God had power to do what He had promised. This is why "it was credited to him as righteousness." The words "it was credited to him" were written not for him alone, but also for us, to whom God will credit righteousness— for us who believe in Him who raised Jesus our Lord from the dead.

Abraham's trial stands out in history like a mountain peak whose height only one other Climber has been called upon to scale: "He who did not spare His own Son, but gave Him up for us all" (Romans 8:32). Abraham is a beautiful type of God the Father. Just as Abraham had an only son, whom he loved, so did God, and He gave His only begotten Son to be slain for us.

God stayed the hand of Abraham before Isaac could be sacrificed. When the Lord Jesus Christ was on the cross upon which He was to be sacrificed, God did not stay His hand! Isaiah 53:10-11 says:

> Yet it was the LORD's will to crush Him and cause Him to suffer, and though the LORD makes His life a guilt offering, He will see His offspring and prolong His days, and the will of the LORD will prosper in His hand. After the suffering of His soul, He will see the light of life and be satisfied; by His knowledge My righteous servant will justify many, and He will bear their iniquities.

Two thousand years after Abraham, One stood in the Temple that crowned Mount Moriah and said, "Abraham rejoiced at the thought of seeing My day; he saw it and was glad" (John 8:56). We believe that it was when Abraham received his son "figuratively speaking . . . back from death" (Hebrews 11:19) that this prophetic rejoicing took place.

It is no wonder that Abraham called this place *Jehovah-jireh,* which means "the LORD will provide" (Genesis 22:14). Some erroneously interpret this name to mean that God will provide for all our needs. This is a comforting truth, but it is not the one taught in the name *Jehovah-jireh.* The reason for this name is given in Genesis 22:14: "On the mountain of the LORD it will be provided." What was it that Abraham saw after he had received Isaac as if from the dead? "Abraham looked up and there in a thicket he saw a ram caught by its horns. He went over and took the ram and sacrificed it as a burnt offering instead of his son" (Genesis 22:13). Years later, John the Baptist exclaimed in joy when he saw Jesus, the Messiah, "Look, the Lamb of God, who takes away the sin of the world!" (John 1:29). Thus, we see another truth in the offering up of Isaac. It is a type of God's provision of a sacrifice. But our Lord Jesus Christ did what Isaac could not do—He became our Sacrifice *for sin.*

Abraham was not the only one whose faith was tested on Mount Moriah. Isaac was a grown man and could easily have resisted his aged father, but he was obedient. We have mentioned that he was not an infant. It takes strength to climb mountains; it takes greater strength to climb mountains carrying wood. How much wood Isaac carried, we do not know, but it was sufficient to bear his body.

Think for a moment of the important effect of this event upon Isaac. From the account in Genesis 22, it seems as if Isaac was ignorant of the fact that he was to be offered up as a sacrifice. Imagine, then how he felt when he was actually tied to the altar and watched as his father reached for his knife! Two thousand years later, One also bore the wood of sacrifice, but He knew what He was doing. He had been born for this very purpose.

The Scriptures do not tell us how Isaac acted when he

was bound to the altar. We have seen him as a robust youth who, as previously mentioned, could have resisted Abraham if he so desired. But he didn't resist. When he allowed himself to be bound and laid upon the altar, he fully entered into the spirit of Abraham; he joined in Abraham's faith. In so doing, he showed himself to be the heir to the promises. How much was the behavior of Isaac like our Lord, who "was oppressed and afflicted, yet He did not open His mouth; He was led like a lamb to the slaughter, and as a sheep before her shearers is silent, so He did not open His mouth" (Isaiah 53:7).

In both Psalm 22 and Luke 22:42-44 we see parallels between the story of Isaac in Genesis 22 and the sacrifice of our Lord. As Isaac lay on the altar and saw the hand of Abraham upraised, certainly he could have wondered, "Father, why have you forsaken me?" But the record is silent. The whole picture given of Isaac shows him in the same attitude as our Lord in Gethsemane, "Not as I will, but as You will" (Matthew 26:39).

The timing of Isaac's sacrifice is also symbolic. When God commanded Abraham to offer up Isaac, he obeyed; and in Abraham's heart, Isaac was dead from that moment on. We should realize that Abraham did not know for sure that God would also "provide a way out" (1 Corinthians 10:13), although he had faith in God's goodness. It was three days later that Isaac was offered, and it was on this third day that Isaac was returned to his father. To some this may seem to be an unimportant detail, but as we saw in Hebrews, chapter 11, Abraham, "figuratively speaking, . . . did receive Isaac back from death." Isaac is clearly a type of the Lord Jesus Christ, who rose on the third day, having yielded up His spirit to the Father. Thus the Father also received His Son on the third day.

God not only "provided a way out" for Abraham; He also provided the lamb for the sacrifice. "Abraham looked up and there in a thicket he saw a ram caught by its horns. He went over and took the ram and sacrificed it as a burnt offering instead of his son" (Genesis 22:13). And thus God the Father has provided us a way of escape from the penalty of sin: "For the wages of sin is death, but the gift of God is eternal life in Christ Jesus our Lord" (Romans 6:23).

This is why the shofar is sounded on Rosh Hashanah.

8

THE DAY OF ATONEMENT: ITS RITUAL

The LORD said to Moses, "The tenth day of this seventh month is the Day of Atonement. Hold a sacred assembly and deny yourselves, and present an offering made to the LORD by fire. Do no work on that day, because it is the Day of Atonement, when atonement is made for you before the LORD your God. Anyone who does not deny himself on that day must be cut off from his people. I will destroy from among his people anyone who does any work on that day. You shall do no work at all. This is to be a lasting ordinance for the generations to come, wherever you live. It is a sabbath of rest for you, and you must deny yourselves. From the evening of the ninth day of the month until the following evening you are to observe your sabbath" (Leviticus 23:26-32).

THERE WERE GOLDEN BELLS on the hem of the high priest's garments. Critics delight to deduce theories from such details and have enjoyed themselves as they proclaim that this proves that Israel's religion was not a revelation from God. They say that all the Jews did was to copy details of contemporary paganism that impressed them. And they "prove their point" by cataloging cases in which pagans wakened their sleeping gods by sounding bells.

All one has to do is to observe that the golden bells on the high priest's garments were not gongs; they were tinkling golden bells. Only a God who was awake and listening would hear them! Thus, the purpose of the bells was not to waken God; it was the people of Israel who needed to hear their music!

God commanded the Israelites in Exodus 28:33-35 to:

Make pomegranates of blue, purple, and scarlet yarn around the hem of the robe, with gold bells between them. The gold bells and the pomegranates are to alternate around the hem of the robe. Aaron must wear it when he ministers. The sound of the bells will be heard when he enters the Holy Place before the LORD and when he comes out, so that he will not die.

When the people heard the sound of the golden bells, they knew that they had a living high priest!

We can understand the importance of having a *living* high priest more easily by observing the somewhat involved ritual of the Day of Atonement as described by Alfred Edersheim.

Seven days before the Day of Atonement the high priest left his own house in Jerusalem, and took up his abode in his chambers in the Temple. A substitute was appointed for him, in case he should die or become Levitically unfit for his duties. Rabbinical punctiliousness went so far as to have him twice sprinkled with the ashes of the red heifer—on the 3rd and the 7th days of his week of separation—in case he had, unwittingly to himself, been defiled by a dead body. During the whole of that week he had to practice the various priestly rites, such as sprinkling the blood, burning the incense, lighting the lamp, offering the daily sacrifice, etc. For, as already stated, every part of that day's services devolved on the high priest, and he must not commit any mistake. Some of the elders of the Sanhedrin were appointed to see to it, that the high priest fully understood, and knew the meaning of the service; otherwise they were to instruct him in it. On the eve of the Day of Atonement the various sacrifices were brought before him, that there might be nothing strange about the services of the morrow. Finally, they bound him by a solemn oath not to change anything in the rites of the day.[1]

Thus, a mistake would be costly. It could mean the life of the high priest, but it could also mean that there would be no atonement for that year.

---

[1]Edersheim, Alfred, *The Temple, Its Ministry and Services*, pp. 268-269.

The Music of the Golden Bells

We should realize three very important facets of the ritual. In the first place, it was only on the Day of Atonement that the high priest was allowed to enter the holy of holies, and on that day he entered the holy of holies four times. Secondly, on these occasions he did not wear the "golden vestments" with the "golden bells." Whenever he entered the holy of holies, he wore white linen garments. Finally, "only while officiating in the distinctly expiatory services of the day did the high priest wear his 'linen garments'; in all the others he was arrayed in his 'golden vestments.' This necessitated a frequent change of dress, and before each he bathed his whole body."[2]

The rituals of the day were detailed and numerous. They began with the regular daily service, which on this day was led by the high priest. He had not slept the night before, and he arrived at the Temple in his ordinary garb. The morning service is described by a Jewish scholar as follows:

First the high priest is conducted to the bath house. The high priest bathes himself five times on this day; in addition, he washes his hands and feet ten times. These bathings and washings are performed in a special room in the Temple, near the court of the priests. The first bath, however, the one in the morning, takes place outside of the innermost court, beyond the water tower.

Each time he bathes a curtain of byssus (costly linen) is spread between him and the people. He doffs his ordinary raiment, bathes, dons the golden vestments, washes his hands and feet in a golden basin, and starts the daily sacrifice. He performs it in his golden robes, and the congregation stands enthralled at the sight. From their point of observation, the high priest is a glowing spectacle, with his golden diadem, the precious gems on his breast, and the golden bells which hang on the hem of his purple robe and which tinkle with every movement that he makes.

He then goes into the anteroom in order to burn the incense on the golden altar, and to put the lamps of the menorah in

---

[2]Ibid., p. 268.

order. This ends the regular daily service; now comes the special Yom Kippur service, for which the high priest dons garments of white linen.

He is led to the bathhouse near the court of the priests. He washes his hands and feet, divests himself of his ceremonial golden robes, bathes himself, puts on the garments of white linen, and again washes his hands and feet.[3]

Each time he changed his raiment, the high priest was separated from the people by a linen cloth. They could not see him, but they could hear "the sound of the bells . . . when he enters the Holy Place" (Exodus 28:35).

Our Great High Priest

Each time the listeners heard the music of the golden bells, their hearts were gladdened by three wonderful truths: (1) they had a living high priest; (2) the high priest was successful in making intercession for them; and (3) their sacrifices had been accepted.

A detailed study of the Day of Atonement would yield a rich harvest, as we would learn of our great High Priest who ever liveth to make intercession for us. For instance, when the high priest entered the court of the Temple clothed in his linen garments, he laid his hands on the head of a young bull and confessed his own sins:

I beseech Thee, O Lord! I have sinned, I have been iniquitous, I have transgressed against Thee, O Lord; pardon the sins, iniquities and transgressions which I have committed against Thee, I and my household, as it is said: "On this day shall atonement be made for you, to cleanse you; from all your sins shall ye be clean before the Lord."[4]

The letter to the Hebrews contrasts our High Priest, Jesus, with the high priest of Israel.

---

[3]Schauss, Hayyim, *The Jewish Festivals*, p. 134.
[4]Ibid., p. 135.

Because of this oath, Jesus has become the guarantee of a better covenant. Now there were many of those priests, since death prevented them from continuing in office; but because Jesus lives forever, He has a permanent priesthood. Therefore He is able to save completely those who come to God through Him, because He always lives to intercede for them. Such a high priest meets our need—One who is holy, blameless, pure, set apart from sinners, exalted above the heavens. Unlike the other high priests, He does not need to offer sacrifices day after day, first for His own sins, and then for the sins of the people (Hebrews 7:22-27).

The high priest's confession was made in the area between the porch of the Temple and the altar. The second part was performed on the eastern side of the altar close to the people. There two goats stood with their heads toward the sanctuary, their backs to the people. Both were of the same size and appearance and cost an equal amount of money. In an urn at their side were two golden tablets that were identical, except that one was inscribed "for Jehovah"; the other, "for Azazel" (the scapegoat). The high priest shook the urn, then thrust both hands into it, withdrew the lots, and laid one on the head of each goat.

The lot having designated each of the two goats, the high priest tied a tongue-shaped piece of scarlet cloth to the horn of the goat for Azazel, the so-called "scapegoat", and another round the throat of the goat for Jehovah, which was to be slain. The goat that was to be sent forth was now turned round towards the people, and stood facing them, waiting, as it were, till their sins should be laid on him, and he would carry them forth into "a land not inhabited." Assuredly a more marked type of Christ could not be conceived, as He was brought forth by Pilate and stood before the people, just as He was about to be led forth, bearing the iniquity of the people. And, as if to add to the significance of the rite, tradition has it that when the sacrifice was fully accepted the scarlet mark which the scapegoat had borne became white, to symbolize the gracious promise in Isaiah 1:18; but it adds that this miracle did not take place for forty years before the destruction of the Temple![5]

---

[5]Edersheim, Alfred, *The Temple, Its Ministry and Services*, p. 273.

Then the high priest sacrificed the young bull; he repeated the same confession, but now he added the sins of the priests, saying, "I and my household and the sons of Aaron, Thy holy tribe." The blood of the bull was gathered in a basin, which was given to a waiting priest, who stirred it so that it would not coagulate.

The high priest then went to the altar of burnt offering, filled a censer of burning coals, scattered frankincense on them, and entered the holy of holies for the first time that day. Filled with fear and awe, the high priest placed the censer of incense on the "foundation stone." The holy of holies was filled with the smoke of the incense. The high priest retired to the holy place, where he prayed. The people in the court also prayed.

The high priest then took the blood of the young bull from the priest, returned to the holy of holies, and sprinkled it toward the place where the mercy seat had been. (In the first Temple, the ark of the covenant was covered by the mercy seat, which was overshadowed by the cloud of glory. However, in Herod's temple there was neither ark nor cloud of glory—all was empty.) When he emerged from the holy of holies, he placed the bowl with the blood of the bullock in front of the veil.

He then sacrificed the goat marked "for Jehovah." Once more he entered the holy of holies and, by a series of sprinklings, ceremonially cleansed the sanctuary, the veil, and the holy place from the defilement of priests and worshipers. As far as the Law could give, there was once more free access to all.

All this time, the scapegoat stood facing the congregation. The high priest, still robed in white (careful, in all of the sprinklings, not to let one drop of blood fall on them), laid his hands on the scapegoat and, instead of saying, "I and my household," he said, "Thy people, the house of Israel" as he prayed for the third time. He turned toward the people and said, "Before the Lord ye shall be clean." Priests led the scapegoat outside the temple area. Hayyim Schauss describes what happened next:

The goat is led to a specified spot about ten miles beyond the city, where a precipitous cliff overhangs a ravine. Prior to Yom Kippur, ten booths were erected as stations along the way. Food and drink are available in each booth for the escorter of the scapegoat, for he may break his fast. A group of Jews escort him from the Temple to the first booth, and in each booth there is somebody to meet him and escort him to the next booth. He is not escorted, however, all the way to the cliff, his escort stopping and watching from afar.

When man and goat come to the cliff, the red sash is removed from the goat's horns and divided in two. One part is attached to the cliff and the other half tied to the horns of the goat, which is then pushed over the cliff, life passing out of him as he falls into the ravine.

The news that the scapegoat is in the wilderness is quickly brought to the high priest.[6]

During the ten mile journey of the scapegoat, the high priest read the *Torah*. When he heard the news that the scapegoat had died "without the camp," he once more bathed and changed his garments. Once more the eager listeners heard the joyful sound of the golden bells.

We who have heard the joyful sound of the golden bells rejoice as we share this wonderful truth with our brethren, "as far as the east is from the west, so far has He removed our transgressions from us" (Psalm 103:12).

---

[6]Schauss, Hayyim, *The Jewish Festivals*, p. 130.

9

THE DAY OF ATONEMENT:
ITS SHORTCOMINGS

When Christ came as high priest of the good things that are already here, He went through the greater and more perfect tabernacle that is not man-made, that is to say, not a part of this creation. He did not enter by means of the blood of goats and calves; but He entered the Most Holy Place once for all by His own blood, having obtained eternal redemption. The blood of goats and bulls and the ashes of a heifer sprinkled on those who are ceremonially unclean sanctify them so that they are outwardly clean. How much more, then, will the blood of Christ, who through the eternal Spirit offered Himself unblemished to God, cleanse our consciences from acts that lead to death, so that we may serve the living God! (Hebrews 9:11-14)

THE DAY OF ATONEMENT is the most sacred day of Israel's calendar. In Old Testament times it was so holy that the ancient Sanhedrin took the greatest care to assure that the high priest would do everything correctly when he ministered in the holy of holies.

We have seen in chapter 8 how carefully the high priest and the Sanhedrin prepared for each ritual on this most holy of holy days. As seen, for seven days before the Day of Atonement, each minute detail was meticulously rehearsed; everything had to be absolutely correct.

The Day of Atonement in the New Testament

It is both significant and ironic that the more correctly the letter of the Law was observed on the Day of Atonement, the more eloquently it testified that it was "weak and useless (for the Law made nothing perfect), and a better hope is introduced, by which we draw near to God" (Hebrews 7:18-19).

In fact, the various offerings on the Day of Atonement were excellent reminders to all of Israel that "the law is only a shadow of the good things that are coming—not the realities themselves. For this reason it can never, by the same sacrifices repeated endlessly year after year, make perfect those who draw near to worship. If it could, would they not have stopped being offered?" (Hebrews 10:1-2). In other words, the law of offerings looked forward to a new and better way.

Levitical high priests, as we have seen, were all weak, mortal, sinful men. Before they could offer a sacrifice for the sins of the people, they had to bring a sacrifice for their own sins. "Aaron is to offer the bull for his own sin offering to make atonement for himself and his household" (Leviticus 16:6).

The Epistle to the Hebrews is the finest explanation of the Day of Atonement. It clearly shows the shortcomings of the Law. It is a commentary on Romans 8:3 and 4: "What the law was powerless to do in that it was weakened by the sinful nature, God did by sending His own Son in the likeness of sinful man to be a sin offering. And so He condemned sin in sinful man, in order that the righteous requirements of the law might be fully met in us, who do not live according to the sinful nature but according to the Spirit."

We should call the Epistle to the Hebrews the "Letter to Hebrew Christians." We do not know who the human author is, nor do we know for certain to whom it was originally addressed. It is possible that it was sent to a group of Jews who had originally been members of a synagogue of the Dispersion. As Jews, they would have

certainly been zealous of the Law. As Jews of the Dispersion, they would also have frequently journeyed to Jerusalem, especially at the Feast of Weeks (Pentecost).

I suggest (please remember, this is just a suggestion) that
this group of Jews may have been among the three thousand Jews of the Dispersion who accepted the Lord on the
Day of Pentecost, or perhaps among the five thousand who
accepted the Lord within a few days after it. In any event,
there is no question that they heard the apostles' preaching
and saw the signs of the power of the Holy Spirit (see
Hebrews 2:3-4). When they returned to their homes their
testimony was probably violently opposed, and they were,
without doubt, expelled from the synagogue. Because of
the persecution they received, they were strongly tempted
to forsake their Lord and return to rabbinical Judaism.

This suggestion concerning those to whom the letter to
the Hebrews was written is just that, a suggestion. However, the existence of such a group of persecuted Hebrew
Christians would explain many of the arguments and most
of the very strong exhortations in this eloquent letter.

To the author of the book of Hebrews, the Day of
Atonement demonstrated the truth that all the sacrifices
of the Law could not have an eternal effect on the problems of forgiveness and atonement. At best, when the high
priest announced, "Ye shall be clean," it was only for a
year. Only the Lord Jesus Christ, Israel's eternal High
Priest, could say, "I give them eternal life, and they shall
never perish; no one can snatch them out of My hand"
(John 10:28). Even at the altar of burnt offering, the peni-
tent Israelite stood afar off, unable to approach the presence of God, who reigned between the cherubim in the
holy of holies within the veil.

The Levitical high priests were weak, sinful men, who
had to be cleansed from sin before they could offer the sin
offering for Israel. Even the Tabernacle, which was minutely described by Moses, was only a copy of the "true tabernacle set up by the Lord, not by man" (Hebrews 8:2).
Levitical sacrifices were sacrifices of animals which could
not remove sin (Hebrews 10:1-4).

Our High Priest

The letter to the Hebrews clearly warned the Hebrew Christians who were being tempted to return to rabbinical Judaism that such an act would be utterly disastrous! It explained that Israel's celebration of the Day of Atonement, according to the author, was just a shadow of the real atonement. Why should they revert to the shadow when in the Lord Jesus Christ they had the reality? The Lord Jesus Christ was a better High Priest than the Levitical priesthood, because unlike them He did not need to offer a sin offering. He was also a better High Priest than the Levitical priests, who were unable to continue in office because they inevitably died. We find these truths expressed in Hebrews 7:24-27:

> But because Jesus lives forever, He has a permanent priesthood. Therefore He is able to save completely those who come to God through Him, because He always lives to intercede for them. Such a high priest meets our need—One who is holy, blameless, pure, set apart from sinners, exalted above the heavens. Unlike the other high priests, He does not need to offer sacrifices day after day, first for His own sins, and then for the sins of the people. He sacrificed for their sins once for all when He offered Himself.

The Levitical sacrifices were "a shadow of the good things that are coming" (Hebrews 10:1), but they could never remove sin. Even the scapegoat figuratively removed sin from the house of Israel only for one year!

The Levitical priests served in the Tabernacle, but as wonderfully symbolic and as highly ornate as that Tabernacle was, it was only a model, not the real thing! Hebrews 8:1-2 makes this truth clear:

> The point of what we are saying is this: We do have such a high priest, who sat down at the right hand of the throne of the Majesty in heaven, and who serves in the sanctuary, the true tabernacle set up by the Lord, not by man.

On the Day of Atonement, the high priest offered sacrifices of animals. The sacrifices obtained forgiveness for sin for a year, but they could never remove sin, "because it is impossible for the blood of bulls and goats to take away sins" (Hebrews 10:4). How much better is the Lord Jesus Christ, our great High Priest! He did what no Levitical high priest was able to do. As a Man, He was without sin; He did not need to offer a sacrifice for His sin. He was able to offer His sinless human life as a sin offering for others. Because He was God and Man, He was both Priest and Victim. As One who conquered death, He offered Himself as our atonement on the cross.

In the old covenant, the veil shut men out of the holy of holies (Hebrews 9:3). The way into the presence of God was not yet opened (Hebrews 9:8). As soon as our Lord died, "the curtain of the temple was torn in two from top to bottom" (Mark 15:38). He entered into the true sanctuary, "He entered heaven itself, now to appear for us in God's presence" (Hebrews 9:24). When He did this, He was invited to occupy the throne at God's right hand. As High Priest, accepted Victim, and accomplished Victor, He invites us to join Him in the presence of God. "Let us then approach the throne of grace with confidence, so that we may receive mercy and find grace to help us in our time of need" (Hebrews 4:16).

10

ISRAEL'S FUTURE DAY OF ATONEMENT

And I will pour out on the house of David and the inhabitants of Jerusalem a spirit of grace and supplication. They will look on Me, the One they have pierced, and mourn for Him as one mourns for an only child, and grieve bitterly for Him as one grieves for a firstborn son. On that day the weeping in Jerusalem will be great, like the weeping of Hadad Rimmon in the plain of Megiddo (Zechariah 12:10-11).

THERE IS A FUTURE DAY OF ATONEMENT for Israel. In chapter 8 we studied the ritual of this most important holy day, also called Yom Kippur. We saw in chapter 9 that the New Testament interprets both the ritual and some of the sacrifices of this day as types of the atoning work of our Lord Jesus Christ. He is called our "great High Priest." The blood of the bulls and goats which was shed on Yom Kippur was a type of the blood shed on Calvary, where our Lord "offered for all time one sacrifice for sins" (Hebrews 10:12). The ritual of the Day of Atonement is rich in symbolic truth.

The rituals and sacrifices of the Day of Atonement also abound in prophetic truth. There are two chapters in Leviticus that teach about this holy day. Chapter 16 describes the ritual, which provides such abundant symbolic truth. However, it is in chapter 23 of Leviticus, which outlines Israel's sacred calendar, that we see the prophetic truth that there is to be a future Day of Atonement for Israel.

The tenth day of this seventh month is the Day of Atonement. Hold a sacred assembly and deny yourselves [afflict your souls, KJV], and present an offering made to the LORD by fire. Do no work on that day, because it is the Day of Atonement, when atonement is made for you before the LORD your God. Anyone who does not deny himself on that day must be cut off from his people. I will destroy from among his people anyone who does any work on that day. You shall do no work at all. This is to be a lasting ordinance for the generations to come, wherever you live. It is a sabbath of rest for you, and you must deny yourselves. From the evening of the ninth day of the month until the following evening you are to observe your sabbath (Leviticus 23:27-32).

A comparison of the two chapters is helpful. In chapter 16, which typifies the work of our Lord, there is very little said about "denying oneself " or the "affliction of the soul" (KJV). This chapter deals primarily with ritual which has been prophetically fulfilled by our Lord. It is also significant that for almost two thousand years, it has been impossible for Israel to perform that ritual. In chapter 23, however, almost none of the rituals are mentioned, but there is repeated emphasis on self-denial, or the affliction of the soul. Thus Israel's future Day of Atonement will be a day of "affliction of the soul."

Forgiveness for the Nation of Israel

It must be borne in mind that the biblical Day of Atonement was for the forgiveness of sins, especially for the nation of Israel rather than the individual Israelite. It was Israel's national day of reconciliation. The central thought of the day's ceremony was not just expiation, it was the complete removal of the sins of the nations. As we see later in this chapter, Israel's future Day of Atonement will bring the Jews as a nation to repentance and forgiveness of sins which hindered them from fellowship with God.

In previous chapters, we observed that all the feasts in Leviticus 23 were prophetic: the Feasts of Passover and Unleavened Bread looked forward to Christ, "our Passover lamb [who] has been sacrificed" (1 Corinthians 5:7). The Feast of Firstfruits was fulfilled in our Lord's resurrection: "But Christ has indeed been raised from the dead, the firstfruits of those who have fallen asleep" (1 Corinthians 15:20). The Feast of Pentecost pointed to the spiritual reaping of the Lord's harvest, to the bringing of salvation to the Gentiles.

It is clear from the Scriptures that these three festivals, all of which occurred in the spring months of the year, were prophetic and that they have already been fulfilled in the death, resurrection, and ascension of our Lord. From this evident truth we may safely infer that the other festivals, which occurred in the fall of the year, the seventh month of Israel's sacred calendar, must also be prophetic.

The significance of the three holy days of the seventh month must be interpreted in the light of those that have already been fulfilled. Besides this, since the Feast of Trumpets, the Day of Atonement, and the Feast of Tabernacles are all celebrated in the seventh month, which is the last month of the sacred calendar as found in Leviticus 23, we will find their fulfillment in the "last times."

Keeping these truths in mind, we may infer that since Pentecost typified the firstfruits of the world's harvest when an election from among all nations was reaped, the Feast of Tabernacles then typifies the completion of that harvest. But between the Feast of Trumpets, which as we have already seen is the rapture, and the Feast of Tabernacles which is the reign of our Lord, is the great tribulation, near the close of which will be Israel's great Day of Atonement.

Zechariah vividly pictures that great day. "I will gather all the nations to Jerusalem to fight against it; the city will be captured, the houses ransacked, and the women raped. Half of the city will go into exile, but the rest of the people will not be taken from the city" (Zechariah 14:2).

We are now living in the only time in world history when this verse can be fulfilled in a very short time. In recent years, the United Nations has generally been united against Israel. Until now this organization of "all the nations" against Jerusalem has been political. However, as I write this, "peace-keeping" troops of the United Nations are gathered within one hundred miles of Israel!

From Zechariah's description, it is clear that initially the United Nations' armies will be victorious. "The city will be captured, the houses ransacked, and the women raped. Half of the city will go into exile, but the rest of the people will not be taken from the city." It is significant that Jerusalem is divided: It is half Arab (East Jerusalem) and half Israeli (West Jerusalem). "Half of the city will go into exile." There is only one suitable staging area in Jerusalem where such a large number of captives could be held until shipped to prison camps. It is the Temple Mount, from which people walking on the Mount of Olives can be distinctly seen.

It is then when it would seem that Jerusalem is utterly defeated by the nations of the world and that the prince of this world is finally victorious. But "then the LORD will go out and fight against those nations," and He shall be victorious. "On that day His feet will stand on the Mount of Olives, east of Jerusalem" (Zechariah 14:3-4). Note the words, "His feet will stand." Why are His feet mentioned? Wouldn't the statement, "He shall stand upon the Mount of Olives" be sufficient? The answer is found in Zechariah 12:9-11:

On that day I will set out to destroy all the nations that attack Jerusalem. And I will pour out on the house of David and the inhabitants of Jerusalem a spirit of grace and supplication. They will look on Me, the one they have pierced, and mourn for Him as one mourns for an only child, and grieve bitterly for Him as one grieves for a firstborn son. On that day the weeping in Jerusalem will be great.

It is Israel's great Day of Atonement! We now see why Zechariah emphasized "His feet" (Zechariah 14:4). Throughout the ages of eternity, our Lord will carry on His body the marks of His love to all men. "They will look on Me, the one they have pierced, and mourn for Him." Just as doubting Thomas became believing Thomas when he saw our Lord's wounds, so rebellious Israel will look at His pierced hands and feet and realize that He alone is the One who was prophesied by Zechariah. "On that day a fountain will be opened to the house of David and the inhabitants of Jerusalem, to cleanse them from sin and impurity" (Zechariah 13:1). It will be a day of "affliction of the soul."

On her great Day of Atonement, Israel's penitential prayer will be Isaiah 53:3-12:

He was despised and rejected by men (verse 3).
Surely He took up our infirmities and carried our sorrows (verse 4).
But He was pierced for our transgressions, He was crushed for our iniquities (verse 5).
The Lord has laid on Him the iniquity of us all (verse 6).
He was led like a lamb to the slaughter (verse 7).
For He was cut off from the land of the living (verse 8).
For the transgression of My people He was stricken (verse 8).
He was assigned a grave with the wicked, and with the rich in His death (verse 9).
And though the LORD makes His life a guilt offering, He will see His offspring and prolong His days (verse 10).
He will bear their iniquities (verse 11).
For He bore the sin of many, and made intercession for the transgressors (verse 12).

It is Israel's High Priest, who has left the holy of holies in the heavens to return, clothed in His robes of righteousness. It is Israel's great Day of Atonement. The Feast of Tabernacles will soon follow.

11

THE FEAST OF TABERNACLES

The LORD said to Moses, "Say to the Israelites: 'On the fifteenth day of the seventh month the LORD's Feast of Tabernacles begins, and it lasts for seven days. The first day is a sacred assembly; do no regular work. For seven days present offerings made to the LORD by fire, and on the eighth day hold a sacred assembly and present an offering made to the LORD by fire. It is the closing assembly; do no regular work' " (Leviticus 23:33-36).

T HE MOST JOYFUL of Israel's festivals was the Feast of Tabernacles. It came at the end of the harvest when the hearts of the people were naturally gladdened. The crops had been reaped. As they looked around them, they remembered that six months before, at passover time, they had dedicated the entire harvest to the Lord by the offering of firstfruits, and now not only were their barns full, their hearts were overflowing with joy and thanksgiving.

But that was not all. As they looked around on the goodly land, the fruits of which had just enriched them, they must have remembered that by miraculous interposition the Lord their God had brought them to this land and given it them, and that He ever claimed it as peculiarly His own. For the land was strictly connected with the history of the people; and both the land and the history were linked with the mission of Israel. If the beginning of the harvest had pointed back to the birth of Israel in their Exodus from Egypt, and forward to the true Passover-sacrifice in the future; if the corn harvest was connected with the giving of the law on Mount Sinai in the past, and the outpouring of the Holy Spirit on the Day of Pentecost; the harvest thanksgiving of the Feast of Tabernacles reminded Israel, on the one hand, of their dwelling in booths in the wilderness, while on the other hand, it pointed to the final harvest when Israel's mission should be completed, and all nations gathered unto the Lord.[1]

The Feast of Tabernacles is two weeks after Rosh Hashanah. It is always on the same day of the week as New Year's Day. A pious Jew began his preparation for the festival as soon as the Day of Atonement was over. He had only five days to erect a *sukkah,* a booth in which he and his family would dwell during the feast.

The Feast of Booths

Historically, Tabernacles looked backward to the Exodus when Israel lived in booths. "Live in booths for seven days: All native-born Israelites are to live in booths so your descendants will know that I had the Israelites live in booths when I brought them out of Egypt. I am the LORD your God" (Leviticus 23:42-43).

Each family built a *sukkah,* which was actually a temporary outdoor structure. It had a twofold purpose: to remind the Jews of their Exodus and to indicate the transitoriness of human life. The roof was made of slats placed closely to one another so that the shade inside the *sukkah* was greater than the light. The roof had to rest on the walls; it could not be fastened. It was then thatched with green branches, and the entire room, walls, and ceiling decorated with flowers and fruit.

Every male who attends an Orthodox synagogue during Tabernacles (*Sukot*) carries with him what is called "the four species": an *etrog,* which is a citron, in his left hand; the *lulav,* a palm branch, in his right hand; two myrtle twigs and two willow branches are bound to the palm branch. The Scriptures state, "On the first day you are to take

[1]Edersheim, Alfred, *The Temple, Its Ministry and Services,* pp. 232-233.

choice fruit from the trees, and palm fronds, leafy branches and poplars, and rejoice before the LORD your God for seven days" (Leviticus 23:40).

Sukot not only looked back into history, it also looked forward into the future when God's promise to Abraham will be fulfilled, when "all peoples on earth will be blessed through you" (Genesis 12:3).

The Feast of Tabernacles was the last of the three festivals when all adult men of ancient Israel thronged Jerusalem. "Three times a year all your men must appear before the LORD your God at the place He will choose: at the Feast of Unleavened Bread, the Feast of Weeks, and the Feast of Tabernacles. No man should appear before the LORD empty-handed: Each of you must bring a gift in proportion to the way the LORD your God has blessed you" (Deuteronomy 16:16-17).

The *Mishnah* gives us a vivid picture of these pilgrimages. From all over the land, all roads were thronged with gaily clad people keeping the holy days. Everybody carried his offering to the Lord. There were olives, dates, pomegranates, wheat, barley, and perhaps a pigeon or turtledove. The rich brought more, the poor less. Those who could, brought their offering in carts, heavily laden with gifts; the poor carried theirs in wicker baskets; but each brought a gift in proportion to the way the Lord God blessed him.

As the pilgrims journeyed, they sang the songs of Zion, the psalms. On one side of the road, a family would sing from Psalm 121: "I lift up my eyes to the hills." Across the road, the response would come: "Where does my help come from?" And all together: "My help comes from the LORD, the maker of heaven and earth."

Others would sing: "I rejoiced with those who said to me, 'Let us go to the house of the LORD.' Our feet are standing in your gates, O Jerusalem. Jerusalem is built like a city that is closely compacted together. That is where the tribes go up, the tribes of the LORD, to praise the name of the LORD according to the statute given to Israel" (Psalm 122:1-4).

It was *Sukot,* the Feast of Tabernacles. The tribes of Israel, their hearts overflowing with praise to the Lord, were going up to Jerusalem to render unto Him honor and praise and glory.

Every *Sukot* service in the Temple not only looked backward in history, it looked forward in prophecy. God had spoken to Abram from Ur of the Chaldees and promised him, "All peoples on earth will be blessed through you" (Genesis 12:3), and the temple service proclaimed this truth.

The services of the week were elaborate; in all there were seventy bullocks that were sacrificed. According to the *Talmud,* there were seventy nations in the world, and a bullock was slain each year during the Feast of Tabernacles for each of them. The ancient rabbis realized a wonderful truth about the prophetic message of *Sukot:* "Then the survivors from all the nations that have attacked Jerusalem will go up year after year to worship the King, the LORD Almighty, and to celebrate the Feast of Tabernacles" (Zechariah 14:16).

The seventh and last day of the feast is a very special day. It is called *Hoshana Rabba,* "the great Hoshana." In the synagogue during the morning service after seven circuits are made around the altar with the *lulav* (palm branches), they are beaten on the floor of the synagogue or its furniture while the worshipers are chanting, "the voice announcing the coming of the Messiah is heard."[2]

This beating of the branches is work which is illegal on the Sabbath. It is for this reason that "the calendar was fixed in such a way that the New Year would not occur on a Sunday so that *Hoshana Rabba* should not fall on the Sabbath which would cause the taking of the willow to be cancelled.[3]

---

[2] *Succot* (anonymous publication by the Union of Orthodox Jewish Congregations Rabbinical Council of America) p. 10.

[3] *The Encyclopedia Judaica,* "Hoshana Rabba," vol. 8, p. 1027.

How Jesus Kept the Feast

One of the ceremonies of the *Sukot* service was the libation of water procession each morning. Abraham Millgram aptly describes this ceremony:

> The water was brought in a golden flask from the fountain of Siloam and poured by the officiating *kohen* into the basin near the altar. This was the most joyous of the temple ceremonies. The *Mishnah* says that "he who has not seen the rejoicing at the place of water-drawing has never seen rejoicing in his life" (Sukkah 5:1). The ceremony was accompanied by a torch-light procession, dances, singing and chanting by the Levitical choir of the fifteen pilgrim psalms, the songs of ascents (Psalms 120—134), to the accompaniment of musical instruments. . . . It was a symbolic act performed in compliance with the prophetic verse, "With joy shall ye draw water out of the wells of salvation" (Isaiah 12:3).[4]

Picture this scene from the life of Jesus: It was *Hoshana Rabba,* on the last and greatest day of the Feast. See the crowds in the temple courts, watch the white-robed priests as they climb the steep ascent from Siloam to the Temple. They are carrying a golden vase of the water they just drew with joy from the well of Siloam. The water was poured into the basin near the altar. Then, as the priest stood with his empty flask, a Man who had been watching cried with a loud voice: "If a man is thirsty, let him come to Me and drink. Whoever believes in Me, as the Scripture has said, streams of living water will flow from within him" (John 7:37-38).

These were strange words to say, anywhere, at any time. But in the Temple on *Hoshana Rabba,* they were not just strange, they were audacious. The entire libation-of-water ceremony celebrated God's provision of life-giving water to the Israelites when they were dying of thirst in the wilderness. "If a man is thirsty, let him come to Me and drink." Our Lord was claiming that the miracle in the

---

[4]Millgram, Abraham, *Jewish Worship,* p. 204.

wilderness, when the rock gushed forth water, pointed to Himself! This is one of the messages of John's Gospel, where we also find our Lord claiming to be the fulfillment of other incidents under the Law: Jacob's ladder, the brazen serpent in the wilderness, and the manna.

There is a future Feast of Tabernacles that is described in the New Testament:

And I heard a loud voice from the throne saying, "Now the dwelling of God is with men, and He will live with them. They will be His people, and God Himself will be with them, and be their God. He will wipe every tear from their eyes. There will be no more death or mourning or crying or pain, for the old order of things has passed away." He who was seated on the throne said, "I am making everything new!" Then He said, "Write this down, for these words are trustworthy and true." He said to me: "It is done. I am the Alpha and the Omega, the Beginning and the End. To him who is thirsty I will give to drink without cost from the spring of the water of life" (Revelation 21:3-6).

Christ our Passover became Christ the Firstfruits from the dead. At Pentecost, the firstfruits of Israel's ripened harvest were presented to the Lord. The first sheaves were reaped from Israel. But Israel did not keep the harvest to herself. The gospel, which was to the Jew first, has been proclaimed to the uttermost parts of the earth. It has been a long time since Pentecost, and we longingly listen for the sound of the trumpet, the return of our Lord. Then after that we look for Israel's Day of Atonement and the nations of our Lord keeping the Feast of Tabernacles.

After this I looked and there before me was a great multitude that no one could count, from every nation, tribe, people, and language, standing before the throne and in front of the Lamb. They were wearing white robes and were holding palm branches in their hands. And they cried out in a loud voice: "Salvation belongs to our God, who sits on the throne, and to the Lamb" (Revelation 7:9-10).

It's *Hoshana Rabba,* the great day of the feast!

12

THE FEAST OF PURIM

Mordecai recorded these events, and he sent letters to all the Jews throughout the provinces of King Xerxes, near and far, to have them celebrate annually the fourteenth and fifteenth days of the month of Adar as the time when the Jews got relief from their enemies, and as the month when their sorrow was turned into joy and their mourning into a day of celebration. He wrote them to observe the days as days of feasting and joy and giving presents of food to one another and gifts to the poor (Esther 9:20-22).

IN ADDITION TO THE FEASTS AND FASTS in Israel's prophetic calendar outlined in Leviticus 23, there are other holidays that have been celebrated by the Jewish people from biblical times until now. The best known of these is the Feast of Purim, that is, the "Feast of Lots," which is frequently known as the Feast of Esther. This day is observed in memory of the preservation of the Jewish nation in the time of Esther. The Hebrew word *purim* comes from a word meaning "lot." Haman cast a lot to determine the day when the Jews would perish (Esther 3:7); thus the festival is called Purim. There is little doubt that Purim was the "feast of the Jews" that our Lord observed when He "went up to Jerusalem" in John 5:1 and at which He healed the impotent man at the pool of Bethesda.

The Story of Esther

In order to really enjoy the story of Purim, you should read through the book of Esther in one sitting. It opens with a feast given by Ahasuerus (whom scholars identify as Xerxes, the son of Hystaspes). His empire consisted of 127 provinces from "India to Ethiopia." Nobles and princes from all over the world attended the banquet. When the festivities reached their climax, the king ordered Queen Vashti to appear before this huge crowd to display her beauty. She refused and was deposed.

A search for a new queen was instituted. Esther, a young Jewish girl of great beauty, was discovered. She was brought to the palace by Mordecai, her kinsman. Esther pleased the king and became the queen of the realm. Meanwhile, Mordecai "was sitting at the king's gate" and learned of a plot to slay the king. He warned Esther, and they saved the king's life. This fact was recorded in the king's chronicles and then promptly forgotten.

Meanwhile, the wicked Haman was promoted and demanded that "every knee" should bow to him. Mordecai the Jew refused to bend his knee to anyone but God. Haman wanted to destroy not only Mordecai but all the Jews. He persuaded the king to authorize their annihilation. Mordecai then pleaded with Esther to intercede with the king on the Jews' behalf and warned her not to refuse: "For if you remain silent at this time, relief and deliverance for the Jews will arise from another place, but you and your father's family will perish. And who knows but that you have come to royal position for such a time as this?" (Esther 4:14)

It was a tough assignment for Esther, but she met the challenge. She devised an ingenious plan. She invited both the king and Haman to a banquet. At this banquet, she asked both of them to come to another banquet. Both the king and Haman gladly accepted the invitation. Haman went home from the banquet "happy and in high spirits. But when he saw Mordecai at the king's gate and observed that he neither rose nor showed fear in his presence, he was filled with rage against Mordecai" (Esther 5:9). He built a gallows about seventy-five feet high, and he couldn't wait for dawn to come "to speak to the king about hanging Mordecai on the gallows he had erected for him" (Esther 6:4).

"That night the king could not sleep" (Esther 6:1). As we now look back, Jewish history, world history, and even redemption history hung, humanly speaking, on one slim thread, "the king could not sleep." The king, who is described in history as "the mighty king, king of kings, king of populous countries, king of this great and mighty earth, far and near," was the mighty king, but he could not sleep. One mightier than he was tossing him about. The king, who could command countless legions, could not command his tired eyelids to close in sleep.

The King Could Not Sleep

He was a vain man. He could not sleep, but at least he could listen to what the historians had recorded about him. He decided to refresh himself with the stories of his brilliant exploits. "So he ordered the book of the chronicles, the record of his reign, to be brought in and read to him" (Esther 6:1). As the pleasant records of his achievements were read to King Ahasuerus, his sleepiness departed. One item startled him. Some enemies had plotted against him, and that plot had been foiled by the wariness of Mordecai, the same Jew Haman couldn't wait to hang on his huge gallows.

" 'What honor and recognition has Mordecai received for this?' the king asked. 'Nothing has been done for him,' his attendants answered" (Esther 6:3).

Mordecai the Jew had saved the king's life, and no one had rewarded him. This troubled the king. Meanwhile, the first rays of sunshine were flooding the court. The king looked out and saw a man approaching. "The king said, 'Who is in the court?' " (Esther 6:4).

Now Haman had just entered the outer court of the palace to speak to the king about hanging Mordecai on the gallows he had erected for him. His attendants answered, "Haman is standing in the court." "Bring him in," the king ordered (Esther 6:4-5).

So Haman came in. He undoubtedly thought the king's invitation would lead to the granting of his desire. However, instead of hanging Mordecai, the king ordered Haman to lead Mordecai in pomp and circumstance through the streets of Shushan. The one who arrogantly strutted into the presence of the king departed leading the horse on which Mordecai rode. Haman entered the palace cursing the Jew; he left it proclaiming of Mordecai, "This is what is done for the man the king delights to honor!" (Esther 6:9)

Enemies of biblical revelation hate the book of Esther. Even conservative scholars question its authenticity. Martin Luther went so far as to say that he wished it did not exist. One of the objections to the book is the fact that God is not mentioned in it. It is true that the name of God is absent from the book, but the power of God is evident on every page of it. A young child reading this story will easily see the hand of God. Read it again and again, and see how all the seeming accidents—the anger of Ahasuerus against Vashti (Esther 2:1), the sleepless night of the king (6:1), the delay in the casting of the lot (3:7; 9:24-32) for eleven months—together demonstrated the power of God just as surely as the parting of the Red Sea or the thunder of Sinai. From whom did timid Esther receive her strength and courage when she said, "I will go to the king. . . . And if I perish, I perish" (4:16)? She didn't name God but she did honor Him. Her faith in God was implicit in her actions.

How utterly futile are the cunningly devised plans of those who plot against the God of Israel! When Haman gloated that he alone was invited to the queen's banquet, he never dreamed he was going to his death. He built a gallows for Mordecai, but was hanged on it himself. Haman sought to destroy the Jews. Instead, he was the means of winning many converts to Judaism: "And many people of other nationalities became Jews" (Esther 8:17). The rabbis say, "The lot is thrown by man but God brings the decision." It is true that the name of God is not in the book of Esther, but the power of God is on every page.

The Purim of the Future

"That night the king could not sleep" (Esther 6:1). Is there not another King who keeps constant vigil? "He who watches over Israel will neither slumber nor sleep" (Psalm 121:4). This King needs no book to remind Him of His own acts. As He keeps vigil, He knows about the Jewish people, of which Mordecai the Jew is a type, who ever sit at His gate. They sat there for ages. They performed a great service for the King!

"What advantage, then, is there in being a Jew, or what value is there in circumcision? Much in every way! First of all, they have been entrusted with the very words of God" (Romans 3:1-2). The Jew spread the knowledge of the King, about His holiness and His goodness. He has informed all the nations about Him. And for this, what has been done to him? He has been hated and persecuted, driven and hunted. He has been the butt of the Hamans of all ages.

This will not always be so. The book of Esther is not only history; it is also prophecy. It teaches the great fact that the Jewish nation, scattered over the face of the earth, is always the object of God's gracious care. He jealously watches over them and protects them, and in His own way delivers them from their enemies. A. C. Gaebelein writes about the last "Haman" to be overthrown:

In Mordecai's exaltation as given in this chapter, in Haman's possession handed over to the Queen and her uncle, and in the authority which both received, we have a fine foreshadowing of what will take place when the final Haman is overthrown. That will be when the times of the Gentiles are passed and the King, our Lord, has come back. Then Israel will get her great blessings, promised long ago by a covenant-keeping God.[1]

---

[1]Gaebelein, A.C., *The Annotated Bible*, "The Book of Esther," p. 116; *Gaebelein's Concise Commentary on the Whole Bible*, p. 416.

The book of Esther instructs the Jews to observe Purim as "days of feasting and joy and giving presents of food to one another and gifts to the poor" (Esther 9:22). One of these "presents of food" associated with Purim is a special delicacy eaten by the Jews. It is called *hamantaschen*. It is a triangular piece of pastry filled with poppy seeds. Its name comes from two German words, *mohn* (poppy seed) and *taschen* (pockets). Because of its association with the Feast of Purim, however, *mohntaschen* came to be called *hamantaschen,* recalling the enemy of the Jews in Persia.

There is a story (undoubtedly apocryphal) about a Jew who attended one of Hitler's Munich rallies at the start of the Nazi coup. While Hitler ranted, cursing the Jews, he became confused by a man in the front row who was laughing in derision at the fuehrer. When the speech was over, Hitler's men detained the heckler and brought him to Hitler, who asked the man who he was.

"I am a Jew," he said proudly.

"Don't you believe that I will carry out my threats to destroy all Jews? This is not a laughing matter," said Hitler.

"You are not the first ruler who sought to destroy us," said the Jew. "Once Pharoah wanted us slain, and now every year at Passover we eat matzahs. Later Haman tried to annihilate us; now each year we eat the delicious *hamantaschen*. I couldn't help laughing, Herr Hitler, while I listened to your ranting. I was wondering what delicacy we will eat and what holiday we will celebrate to commemorate your downfall."

There will be a Purim in the future. What happened to the enemies of the Jews in Shushan will be the lot of all who hate them. "No weapon forged against you will prevail, and you will refute every tongue that accuses you" (Isaiah 54:17). This is God's promise.

13

HANUKKAH

... [Those] who shut the mouths of lions, quenched the fury of the flames, and escaped the edge of the sword; whose weakness was turned to strength; and who became powerful in battle and routed foreign armies. Women received back their dead, raised to life again. Others were tortured and refused to be released, so that they might gain a better resurrection. Some faced jeers and flogging, while still others were chained and put in prison. They were stoned; they were sawed in two; they were put to death by the sword. They went about in sheepskins and goatskins, destitute, persecuted and mistreated—the world was not worthy of them. They wandered in deserts and mountains, and in caves and holes in the ground. These were all commended for their faith, yet none of them received what had been promised (Hebrews 11:33-39).

HANUKKAH is a post-Mosaic Jewish holy day. It is not mentioned in the Old Testament, but it is mentioned by name in the New Testament: "Then came the Feast of Dedication at Jerusalem. It was winter, and Jesus was in the temple area walking in Solomon's Colonnade" (John 10:22-23). The margin reference to verse 22 explains that the Feast of Dedication was Hanukkah. This indicates that our Lord celebrated Hanukkah. As we shall see, He also used its history in the Olivet Discourse when He answered His disciples' question, "What will be the sign of Your coming and of the end of the age?" (Matthew 24:3)

There is another interesting observation about Hanukkah. Even though this festival is not mentioned in the Old Testament, the events of the original Hanukkah are clearly prophesied in the book of Daniel, as we see later in this chapter. It is one of the finest examples of fulfilled prophecy in the Scriptures.

In our Bibles there is a "blank page" between Malachi and Matthew. The casual reader quickly turns this page and hardly realizes that it represents four hundred years of history. Because no prophet arose during these centuries and no inspired writer added one word to the canon of Scripture, Bible scholars frequently refer to them as the four hundred silent years. But God was not silent during these times, and the prophetic Scriptures show that He was not silent about them.

At the close of Old Testament history, Israel was ruled by Persia. Persia allowed the Jews to have a large degree of self-government as well as religious freedom. The Persians permitted the Jews to organize a political commonwealth governed by the high priests. Ezra had given a new significance to the Law when it was read and explained to the whole house of Israel (see Nehemiah 8). Specialists of the Law, known as scribes, devoted themselves to its study and interpretation. The most pious Jews believed that the highest moral accomplishment was the scrupulous observance of every precept.

However, all of this began to change when the Greeks conquered the Persians. Darius III became king of Persia in 336 B.C. In the same year, twenty-year-old Alexander ascended to the throne of Macedonia. His father had commissioned him to destroy the Persian Empire. Three years later, Alexander's armies defeated the Persians at Issus. Two years later, the Persian army was crushed at Arbela.

Alexander the Great in Prophecy

Two centuries before Alexander was born, his biography was written by Daniel:

Then a mighty king will appear, who will rule with great power and do as he pleases. After he has appeared, his empire will be broken up and parceled out toward the four winds of heaven. It will not go to his descendants, nor will it have the power he exercised, because his empire will be uprooted and given to others (Daniel 11:3-4).

Note how accurately each detail of this remarkable prophecy was literally fulfilled. "A mighty king will appear." This was Alexander the Great. He "will rule with great power." A legend states that Alexander wept because he had no more worlds to conquer. He will "do as he pleases." Twice Darius offered to negotiate a very favorable treaty, but Alexander did not want negotiations; he demanded victory. "After he has appeared, his empire will be broken up and parceled out toward the four winds of heaven." When Alexander died at the age of thirty-three, his generals divided the kingdom among themselves: Ptolemy ruled Egypt in the South; Seleucus's empire extended east beyond Babylon; Lysimachus ruled what is now Turkey in the North; and Cassander ruled Greece in the West. (In describing this division, we have used Israel as the hub.) "It will not go to his descendants" and will be "given to others." Alexander had children, but they did not inherit the empire; as noted above, his generals divided it among themselves.

Alexander conquered the world. But he was not only a general; he was a zealous and brilliant apostle of a new religion, Hellenism. He was completely convinced that the Greek religion, Greek philosophy, and Greek culture were the only way of life. He was the "Apostle Paul" of Hellenism. Alexander died, but his religion still flourishes today.

Ancient Israel was a frontier province between Europe, Asia, and Africa. On its Maritime Plain the armies of the nations maneuvered. In its hills and mountains, a people lived who believed in the God of Abraham, Isaac, and Jacob. Hellenism and Judaism had to meet head on. Hanukkah is the story of that struggle and confrontation.

We have noted with what intricate detail Daniel, chapter 11, describes Alexander and his kingdom. That detail continues throughout the chapter as the prophet notes the course of history until finally, a century and half later, a wicked despot is described as "a contemptible person who has not been given the honor of royalty" (Daniel 11:21). This contemptible person was Antiochus Epiphanes. Much of the same "prophetic history" in Daniel 11 is also forecast in Daniel 8:11-14, describing him as follows:

It set itself up to be as great as the Prince of the host; it took away the daily sacrifice from Him, and the place of His sanctuary was brought low. Because of rebellion, the host of the saints and the daily sacrifice were given over to it. It prospered in everything it did, and truth was thrown to the ground. Then I heard a holy one speaking, and another holy one said to him, "How long will it take for the vision to be fulfilled, the vision concerning the daily sacrifice, the rebellion that causes desolation, and the surrender of the sanctuary and of the host that will be trampled underfoot?" He said to me, "It will take 2,300 evenings and mornings; then the sanctuary will be reconsecrated."

The story of Hanukkah is the history of the "2,300 evenings and mornings" until the sanctuary was reconsecrated! We have observed that the Greeks were passionate missionaries who tried to convert the whole world to Greek religion and philosophy. In Israel, the scribes and priests soon saw that they had a rival party, the more liberal Hellenistic Jews. It was not long before Judea became Hellenistic in all phases of its political, social, and religious life. This was the situation when Antiochus Epiphanes deliberately attempted to destroy Judaism by brute force.

When Antiochus was crowned king, the high priest was Onias III, the leader of the old Orthodox party in Judea. The head of the Hellenist party was Onias's brother, Jason. Jason promised Antiochus huge amounts of money to purchase the office of high priest. He said he would then erect a temple to Phallus in Jerusalem, together with a gymnasium. He also promised to enroll the inhabitants of Jerusalem as citizens of Antioch.

Antiochus gladly agreed to everything. Onias was deposed, Jason was appointed as high priest, and the "final solution" was begun. A gymnasium was erected outside the castle; the youths of Jerusalem nakedly performed gymnastics in the sight of the Temple. Priests left their service at the altar to take part in the games. Many Jewish youths surgically removed the traces of circumcision from their bodies. With characteristic liberality, the high priest Jason sent a contribution to the sacrifices in honor of Heracles at the quadrennial festivities in Tyre.

Antiochus felt that the time was ripe to undertake the total eradication of the Jewish religion.

He gave himself the surname *Epiphanes,* which means "the visible god"; in other words, he and Jupiter were to be considered identical. Worse still, he acted as though that was really the case, with the result that people began to call him *Epimanes,* "the madman."[1]

Antiochus had a fixation about the Sabbath and circumcision, so both were forbidden under the penalty of death. Altars to Greek gods were built in all cities of Judea, and pagan sacrifices were offered to them. Once every month searches of homes were instituted. If the officers found a copy of the Scriptures or a youth who had been circumcised, the whole family was slain.

The Abomination of Desolation

In Jerusalem on the fifteenth of Kislev, 168 B.C., Antiochus violated the holy of holies by erecting a pagan altar on the great altar of burnt offerings. Finally, on the twenty-fifth of Kislev, as Solomon Grayzel describes:

In the Temple above the altar was placed a statue of Jupiter bearing an obvious resemblance to Antiochus. Over such a Temple, Menelaus [who supplanted Jason by a larger bribe] consented to remain as high priest. To that statue were brought as sacrifices the animal most detested by the Jews, the pig. An abominable act had been perpetrated on that twenty-fifth day

---

[1]Grayzel, Solomon, *A History of the Jews,* p. 54.

of Kislev in the year 168 B.C.E. and, to use the descriptive expression of the book of Maccabees, it left the Jewish people desolate.[2]

We see in Antiochus Epiphanes, who placed a statue of Jupiter bearing an obvious resemblance to himself "in the Temple above the altar," a prototype of the coming "man of lawlessness . . . [who] sets himself up in God's temple, proclaiming himself to be God" (2 Thessalonians 2:3-4).

Daniel prophesied of him: "His armed forces will rise up to desecrate the temple fortress and will abolish the daily sacrifice. Then they will set up the *abomination that causes desolation*" (Daniel 11:31, italics added).

It looked as if the God of Abraham, Isaac, and Jacob was crushed in defeat. But eighteen hundred years previous to that, God had promised Abraham that "all peoples on earth will be blessed through you" (Genesis 12:3), and four hundred years previous to this time, God had said, "It will take 2,300 evenings and mornings; then the sanctuary will be reconsecrated" (Daniel 8:14).

In the town of Modin, a Syrian officer set up a statue of Jupiter and ordered an aged priest named Mattathias to sacrifice a pig on the altar. The priest refused, and when a renegade stepped forward to sacrifice the pig, Mattathias slew him and the Syrian officer and fled to the mountains with his family. Other brave Jews joined him, and resistance grew into revolution. Antiochus was stunned and sent his ablest general Lysias, to crush the revolt. It looked as if the Jews would be annihilated. Even the faithful were beginning to doubt.

In the Jerusalem hills the Jews prayed, and one of the priests read the book of Daniel. Professor H. Graetz, the prince of Jewish historians, writes as follows:

The book of Daniel half conceals and half reveals, in a sort of allegory, the destruction of the wicked Syrian Empire, which was the heir to former kingdoms. It foretells that the fourth kingdom on earth, following that of the Babylonians, the Medo-Persians and the Macedonians, would utter foolish words against the

---

[2]Ibid., p. 56.

Almighty, seek to destroy the pious and to turn them away from
the festivals and the laws. The pious would fall into its clutches
for "a time, two times, and half a time." Then dominion would
pass into the hands of the people of the Holy One for ever, and
all knees would bow down to Him. In another vision he saw the
fourth Syrian Empire extending far away to the south, to the east
and to the north, rising to the heavens, and casting down stars
unto the earth, and crushing them. It would exalt itself over the
King of heavenly hosts, it would abolish the daily sacrifice, and
set up an idol in the sanctuary. To the question:

*How long shall be the vision concerning the continual burnt-offering
and the transgression that maketh desolate, to give up both the sanctuary
and the host to be trodden under foot?* (Daniel 8:13) a voice answered:

*Unto two thousand and three hundred evenings and mornings; when
the sanctuary shall be justified* (verse 14).

The book of Daniel, with its mystical revelations, was undoubtedly read with great interest by the Assidaeans. The
apocalyptic form, which gave each line a peculiar meaning, and
reflected the present conditions, lent it a great attraction. More-
over, it solved the problem of the present calamities, and showed
the object of the horrible persecutions; these were intended, on
the one hand, to destroy sin, and on the other hand, to ennoble
believers. It was evident that the duration of the period of affliction had been determined from the beginning, and that this very
duration, too, had a secret meaning. The worldly kingdoms
would disappear, and at the end time, God's kingdom, the kingdom of the holy ones, would commence, and those who had died
or had been slain during the persecutions would awake to eternal life. Thus, though no prophet arose, still there existed a
prophecy for the present time.[3]

Although we disagree with Professor Graetz on details
such as the identity of the fourth empire, he has remarkable insight into the Scriptures.

The prophetic Scriptures had their comforting and mo-
tivating effect. The Syrian host expected to annihilate the
Jews but they themselves were annihilated at Emmaus.
The road to Jerusalem and the Temple was open. The
Temple was cleansed, and the God of Israel was once again
worshiped. Beginning with the twenty-fifth day of Kislev,

[3]Graetz, H., *History of the Jews*, vol. 1, pp. 465-466.

the Jews now observe their eight-day Feast of Dedication, also known as Hanukkah or the Feast of Lights.

Antiochus began his persecution of the Jews in 171 B.C., and it was twenty-three hundred days later in December of 165 B.C. that the Temple was cleansed. The Jewish nation was *not* destroyed, and one hundred seventy years later "there were shepherds living out in the fields nearby, keeping watch over their flocks at night. An angel of the Lord appeared to them, and the glory of the Lord shone around them, and they were terrified. But the angel said to them, 'Do not be afraid. I bring you good news of great joy that will be for all the people. Today in the town of David a Savior has been born to you; He is Christ the Lord' " (Luke 2:8-11).

The "centuries of silence" were over. God, who had in times past spoken to our fathers by the prophets, now spoke by His Son.

The Hanukkah of the Future

Just before the earthly ministry of our Lord, Herod the Great repaired and rebuilt the same Temple that had been cleansed on the first Hanukkah. Herod's temple became one of history's most magnificent structures. Then, the week preceding our Lord's death,

Jesus left the temple and was walking away when His disciples came up to Him to call His attention to its buildings. "Do you see all these things?" He asked. "I tell you the truth, not one stone here will be left on another; every one will be thrown down." As Jesus was sitting on the Mount of Olives, the disciples came to Him privately. "Tell us," they said, "when will this happen, and what will be the sign of your coming and of the end of the age?" (Matthew 24:1-3)

In the verses immediately following the discussion with His disciples, Jesus answered the question, "What will be the sign of Your coming and of the end of the age?" He

told them that some of these signs would be wars, international unrest, famines, pestilences, and false messiahs.
These are general signs. There have been few, if any, generations that have not experienced them to some degree.
But there is one specific sign that identifies the end
of the age. "So when you see standing in the holy place 'the
abomination that causes desolation,' spoken of through
the prophet Daniel—let the reader understand—then let
those who are in Judea flee to the mountains" (Matthew
24:15-16).

Our Lord told His disciples that there is to be a Hanukkah of the future. The Hanukkah that our Jewish neighbors
celebrate commemorates the cleansing of the Temple after
it had been defiled by Antiochus Epiphanes in 168 B.C. That
defilement was so great that it is described by the most
disgusting phrase in the Scriptures, "the abomination that
causes desolation."

The Hebrew word for abomination is *shiqquts,* meaning
"filthy."

When Daniel undertook to specify an abomination so surpass-
ingly disgusting to the sense of morality and decency, and so
aggressively against everything that was godly as to drive all
from its presence and leave its abode desolate, he chose this as
the strongest among several synonyms, adding the qualification,
"that maketh desolate."[4]

Our Lord told His disciples that there is to be a Hanukkah of the future. He says that one will arise who is another
Antiochus Epiphanes, the man of sin, or beast (2 Thessalonians 2:3-8). Just as there was a falling away and Antiochus
was a type of the "man of lawlessness" who was to be
revealed, so there will be one who "opposes and exalts
himself over everything that is called God or is worshiped,
and even sets himself up in God's temple, proclaiming
himself to be God" (2 Thessalonians 2:4).

---

[4]*International Standard Bible Encyclopedia,* vol. 1, p. 16.

It will be the return of our Lord in glory that will result in the overthrow of the man of lawlessness and the establishment of the millennial kingdom. "He who testifies to these things says, 'Yes, I am coming soon.' Amen. Come, Lord Jesus" (Revelation 22:20).